MEET THE BILLY GRAHAM
YOU PROBABLY DON'T KNOW:

The boy growing up on a North Carolina dairy farm . . . the teenager racing his father's car on country roads . . . the excellent young Fuller Brush salesman . . . the pastor of a small Baptist church in Illinois . . . the dynamic Youth for Christ organizer . . . the man deeply concerned over racial injustice and the plight of Soviet Jews. . . .

In this new biography, Gerald Strober gives readers new insights into the life of the great twentieth-century evangelist—the man who, more than any other single person, has made evangelical Christianity a respected world view.

More . . .

ABOUT THE AUTHOR

Gerald S. Strober is a prolific author and has been an active political advisor for such people as the late Robert F. Kennedy and Senator Harry M. Jackson. For over five years he served on the Interreligious Affairs staff of the American Jewish Committee and was Executive Chairman of the National Interreligious Task Force on Soviet Jewry. His books include *American Jews: Community in Crisis* and *Portrait of the Elder Brother: Jews and Judaism in Protestant Teaching Materials*.

Gerald Strober

Billy Graham
His Life and Faith

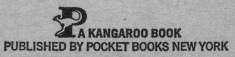
A KANGAROO BOOK
PUBLISHED BY POCKET BOOKS NEW YORK

Distributed in Canada by PaperJacks Ltd., a Licensee
of the trademarks of Simon & Schuster, a division of
Gulf+Western Corporation.

POCKET BOOKS, a Simon & Schuster division of
GULF & WESTERN CORPORATION
1230 Avenue of the Americas, New York, N.Y. 10020
In Canada distributed by PaperJacks Ltd.,
330 Steelcase Road, Markham, Ontario.

Published by arrangement with Word, Inc.
Library of Congress Catalog Card Number: 76-56484

ISBN: 0-671-81890-2

First Pocket Books printing December, 1978

Trademarks registered in the United States and other countries.

PRINTED IN CANADA

*In loving memory
of my mother,
Faye Strober.*

Contents

Part One:

Billy Graham's Career—
Chronological Sequence

Part Two:

Billy Graham and Major Issues

Contents

Part Three:

Billy Graham—
The Man and Evangelical Leader

Preface

I AM very much indebted to a number of individuals in the Billy Graham Evangelistic Association for their aid in assembling material for this book. I should like to particularly thank Drs. Grady and T. W. Wilson, Mr. Don Bailey and Ms. Stephanie Wills. I am, of course, most thankful for the cooperation granted by Dr. Billy Graham, who is one of the finest men I have ever met.

I should also mention my debt to previous writers, especially John Pollock whose book, *Crusades,* is a standard reference on Mr. Graham, and Curtis Mitchell, author of *The Story of the New York Crusade.*

This book owes its beginning to the wise counsel of the late Marie Rodell, and I want to thank my children, Robin, Jonathan and Lori, for their interest.

Prologue

THE GREAT silver and blue aircraft began to slow its speed as it approached Charlotte, North Carolina. In the third seat on the left side of the cabin, a tall, middle-aged man with a handsome tanned face and a full head of greying hair looked down at the city.

"Charlotte has certainly grown since my boyhood days," he remarked to his seatmate. "Why there's the place where my Dad's farm was located. Now it's a shopping center. And look over there where that group of new buildings is. That's where Grady and T. W. Wilson grew up."

It was May, 1975, and Billy Graham, the world's best-known evangelist and a widely admired and respected person, was coming to his hometown to be honored by the dedication of an auditorium in his name. The great religious leader had received many awards in his career, but this was a very special occasion, close to his heart, and as the plane made its final approach to the Charlotte airport, Billy Graham's mind went back over the years to the days when he was a youngster milking cows and helping his father with the many chores that went into the operation of a successful dairy farm.

Part One

Billy Graham's Career–
Chronological Sequence

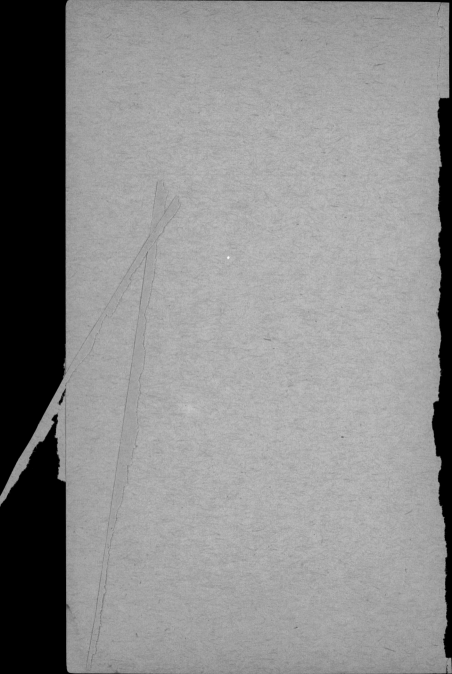

1.

Growing Up in Charlotte

WILLIAM FRANKLIN GRAHAM, JR., was born on November 7, 1918. His ancestry was Scottish—his family came to America in the 1700s, and his grandfather, Crook Graham, was a veteran of the American Civil War. Billy's mother, Morrow Coffey Graham, was a descendant of President James Polk. Billy was the eldest child in a family which would eventually include Catherine, Melvin, and Jean.

In the early twentieth century the southern United States, the region in which Billy was born, was agricultural, tradition-bound, and still smarting from its defeat at the hands of the Union forces in the American Civil War. It was an area filled with racial tension, and the old-time religion was deeply embedded in its very nature. There was little room for new ideas or dissent from the established patterns of doing things, but at the same time, family life was warm and congenial. Billy's parents, like many of their contemporaries, placed a very high value on work, education, and morality. Billy's parents were not strict churchgoers, but they believed in the God of the Bible.

Billy has always had a delightful sense of humor and as a boy, growing up on his father's farm, he enjoyed playing pranks on anyone he could. He was often caught on the wrong end of his father's belt or his mother's long hickory stick. Sometimes he got it for pulling up lettuce heads, and other times it was for teasing his sister Catherine, or playing tricks on his cousins.

There is a famous story that is often told about the time Billy fidgeted too much in church. His father lost his temper and abruptly took Billy to the back of the church and applied an old-fashioned whipping to Billy's backside.

"Billy was rowdy, mischievous," remarked one of his older cousins, "but on the other hand he was soft and gentle and loving and understanding. He was a very sweet, likable person."

When Billy was fifteen his mother, Morrow Graham, began attending a Bible class which measurably strengthened her spiritual life. Billy was a normal, healthy youngster occupied with school and the unending activities of his dad's farm. There was always plenty of work to do, and Billy especially enjoyed working with Reese Brown, the family's black employee, who was one of the strongest and finest men Billy knew during his boyhood.

During his early boyhood days, Billy's chief interest was baseball. He had learned to play the game with the McMakin boys. These were the three sons of the share-cropper on his father's farm. (Mr. McMakin had once been a Southern bicycle racer.)

When Billy was ten years old his father arranged a meeting and a handshake with the immortal baseball great, Babe Ruth. As a high school player at Sharon School, Billy's baseball interest developed but his performance was not that good. He could run, throw, and field, but he was a weak hitter. Nevertheless, he made the Sharon team as a first baseman and dreamed of being a professional, although that dream faded before he finished high school.

During his early teen years Billy showed little evidence of any great interest in religion, although he was friendly with and had great respect for the McMakin brothers, children of the Grahams' intensely religious sharecropper. Billy seemed more interested in racing around the nearby roads in his father's car than he was in religion. One day Billy was out riding with some friends, and as he turned sharply to avoid hitting a car which had veered into his path, his auto ran off the road and into a ditch. Billy called his father, and Frank Graham managed to get the car back on the road, but not before he let Billy know how angry he was.

The September before Billy's sixteenth birthday

Mordecai Ham, a well-known evangelist, came to Charlotte, North Carolina, to hold a series of meetings. Ham, a fiery and outspoken preacher, had been brought to the city by a group of businessmen who hoped to spark a spiritual revival. Billy attended the Ham meetings with his friend, Albert McMakin, and while he found the programs interesting, he did not respond at first to the invitation to come forward and accept Christ as Savior.

Billy did experience a feeling common to many people who attend revival meetings. He thought that the evangelist was looking right at him every time Ham talked about man's sinfulness and inability to please God through his own actions. To escape Mordecai Ham's accusing look Billy joined the choir, even though he had little talent for that role. Although he couldn't see Ham's face from his position in the choir, which was located in back of the platform, he could still hear his voice. Billy stil' remembers how he was struck by Ham's words ar message. "I do remember a great sense of burd that I was a sinner before God and had a great f ir of hell and judgment."

Billy was definitely under conviction, but he uld not as yet bring himself to come forward. Th , one night after Ham preached and the choir s g the old hymn *Almost Persuaded, Christ to Belie e,* Billy felt the presence of Christ and joined with f e group of people who had come forward to star in front of the pulpit. There were no radio micr phones or TV or film cameras present to record ne moment for history. This was simply the case of a teenage boy making a decision at an evangelistic meeting—a common enough happening in the old-time South. Yet it was really an historic moment for this young man who would one day tell more people about Jesus Christ than any other person in history. Several months before when a group of Charlotte businessmen had met to plan the Ham evangelistic campaign, one of the leaders had prayed that God would raise up from Charlotte a man to preach the gospel throughout the world. Although no one in the tabernacle could possibly know it, least of all Billy Graham himself, Billy's conversion marked the first step in the answer to this prayer.

Young Graham's conversion was not as dramatic as St. Paul's experience on the Damascus road. Its character was more of a growing conviction that he was in the will of God and that the sovereign God of the universe had cleansed him from sin and pointed his life in a new and satisfying direction. Like many teenagers who experience the new birth, Billy felt led to undertake formal Bible training, and when he graduated from Sharon High School, he enrolled at Bob Jones College in Cleveland, Tennessee.

2.

Florida Bible Institute

BOB JONES, the founder and president of the school which bears his name, was a famous evangelist and Bible teacher. He was also a strict disciplinarian and a man who had little time for interpretations of Scripture and views of Christian living other than his own. Discipline at his college was very strict, and the students were not encouraged to seek after truth or knowledge by themselves. At first Billy enjoyed life at Bob Jones College. Two of his Charlotte friends, the Wilson brothers—Grady and Thomas Walter (or T. W., as he preferred to be called)—were fellow students. The summer before starting college, the boys, along with Albert Mc-Makin, had worked for the Fuller Brush Company

as traveling salesmen in the South Carolina terri-
tory. Billy was an excellent sales representative.
Even in those days he had a tremendous personality
and was a hard worker. After hours the McMakin
crew would gather for Bible study and prayer, and
these informal but earnest sessions greatly aided
young Graham's early spiritual growth. When Billy's
first college Christmas vacation began he looked
forward to the time away from college with more
enthusiasm than would normally be expected. There
were two reasons for this. He was ill. He had had a
difficult struggle with the flu and needed rest, and
more important, he was beginning to find the atmosphere at Bob Jones College rather oppressive. Billy's
faith was real and growing, but he was intellectually
curious, and his mind was maturing rapidly. Bob
Jones College was not the place for such an inquis-
itive young man. Billy and his parents realized that
a change in school settings was called for. At about
that time Mrs. Graham received some very favor-
able information concerning a small Bible College
in Tampa, Florida. The school was said to have a
fine faculty, a wholesome atmosphere, and what is
more, it seemed an ideal place for Billy to finally
shake off the flu. So in January of 1937, Billy
Graham enrolled at the Florida Bible Institute.

Billy's three years at the Florida Bible Institute
were, on the whole, filled with happy experiences. It
was here that he learned preaching, and at night he
would often go out to an old tree stump on the

campus and practice sermons. He visited some of the
rescue missions and smaller churches in the Tampa
area many times, and he always found a ready response to his messages. While at the Florida Bible
Institute his health improved, and he had the opportunity to meet a number of important Christian laymen who came to the campus to escape the rigors of
the northern winter. One of these lay people, a successful Chicago businessman, influenced Billy to go
to Wheaton College and later helped him with his
first year's tuition.

In the middle of Billy's development at Tampa,
as both a Christian and a young adult, there was
one unhappy episode. He was in love with Emily
Cavanaugh, a fellow student, and during the summer of 1937 the couple became engaged. Later,
however, she was not sure she wanted to marry
Billy, and she asked him to pray for God's guidance.
Emily also sought spiritual help at this time of crisis,
and she finally felt led to break the engagement. On
Class Night, 1938, Billy and a fellow student, Charles
Massey, each purchased corsages for Emily. Emily
wore the flowers offered by Charles, but she returned
Billy's corsage—telling him that she was going to
marry Charles. Billy was upset by this news, but he
returned to the Class Night party as if he didn't
have a care in the world.

Later Emily and Charles became Billy's friends,
and Billy took particular interest in Charles's success
as an army chaplain. Looking back on this difficult

moment in his life Billy later said, "One of two things could happen in a time like that. You can resist and become bitter, or you can let God break you, and I determined to let God have his way."

3.

The Years at Wheaton

Upon graduation from Florida Bible Institute Billy went north to Wheaton College in Illinois for the fall semester of 1940. Anyone waiting at the Wheaton train station on an early September day in 1940 would not have paid much attention to the tall, rangy young man who stepped onto the platform lugging a suitcase, a bag full of books (including a set of encyclopedias he had already read through), and a well-thumbed Bible. He seemed to be just another college kid, perhaps a bit older and more mature looking than average, arriving at a Midwest college for another school year.

In those days Wheaton was a sleepy little town, similar to the many suburban communities which ringed Chicago. Only the college—the town's main industry and point of interest—made Wheaton different. Most of the students lived in dormitories, but some stayed with townsfolk and a few, like Billy, lived in the homes of college professors.

Wheaton College was a highly respected educational institution. It ranked first among the evangelical colleges of its day, and it was noted for a successful blending of rigorous academic pursuit and strong spiritual emphasis. The curriculum at Wheaton centered on the Bible, but there were many hours devoted to history, the sciences, and the performing and graphic arts. Wheaton prepared its students for a lifetime of Christian service. The faculty believed that to be effective in their ministries the students should learn all they could about the world and its peoples. For Graham, Wheaton was an intellectual challenge. His earlier educational training had been much less strenuous and sophisticated, and now he had to devote long hours to study and class preparation.

Still, he found time to lead an active, dynamic spiritual life. At Wheaton Billy was known as a man of prayer, dedicated to soul-winning. Ruth Bell, the lovely daughter of missionaries and the girl who would later marry Billy, recalls the first time she heard his voice. He was praying aloud in a group, and she was struck by his earnest tone as he asked God to bring salvation to people in far-off lands.

Billy also worked at Wheaton. He had a job helping a classmate, Johnny Streator, operate a moving
business. John, who had served in the Navy, ran
the Wheaton College Students Trucking Service. The
Service used a truck Johnny bought for fifty dollars
to pick up the students' baggage from the Aurora
and Elgin railroad stations and the bus terminal. The
Service also hauled furniture on the campus. Johnny
was the person who first told Billy about Ruth Bell
and who actually introduced the couple. One day
as the two friends drove back from the Union Station
Johnny said to Billy, "You must meet the second
nicest girl on campus." (The nicest was Carol Lane,
Johnny's girl.) Billy thought that sounded like a fine
idea, and a day or so later when Johnny spotted
Ruth talking to some friends in front of the college dining hall, he made the fromal introductions.
Johnny, now a pastor in California, recalls that
when Billy and Ruth met, "It was a classic case of
love at first sight." Billy asked Ruth for a date,
and the following Sunday they went to a presentation of Handel's *Messiah*. Later they walked through
a snowstorm and discussed their interests and hopes
for the future. Ruth, whose father was Dr. L. Nelson
Bell, a distinguished medical missionary in China,
planned to serve on the foreign mission field, while
Billy, who was already an experienced and persuasive
preacher, appeared headed for a career in the pulpit
ministry. The couple decided to pray about this

apparent clash in career goals, and after some time Ruth felt God leading her in the direction of accepting Billy's call. In the summer of 1941 they became engaged.

4.

Youth for Christ

UPON GRADUATION from college most young people feel anxious about the future. Some are not quite sure what they want to do, while others worry about finding the right kind of job. The Wheaton College graduating class of 1943 had another major factor with which to contend. The world was at war. That summer German troops were attempting to seize the large Russian city of Stalingrad, while American forces were fighting in North Africa and the Pacific. Many of Billy's classmates were headed for military service, and he seemed destined for the chaplaincy corps. While waiting for his commission to come through, Graham accepted the pastorate of a small Baptist church in Western Springs, Illinois.

That summer Billy and Ruth were married, and Billy worked at building up the membership of his church. In October 1943, Graham received a telephone call from Torrey Johnson, a well-known Chicago pastor. Johnson was the host of a Sunday evening radio program called "Songs in the Night" and was now involved in a new venture. He was about to form an organization called Youth for Christ, and Johnson asked Billy to take over responsibility for his radio program. Billy was flabbergasted by the offer. The show was aired over a major station and cost one hundred dollars a week to maintain. Billy and Ruth prayed over this new opportunity and consulted with their church members. Finally Graham decided to accept Johnson's offer. He went on the air in January of 1944 and was an immediate success. This led Johnson to make another offer; one which would have far-flung consequences beyond anyone's dreams or visions. Johnson asked Billy to work with him in organizing Youth for Christ. Billy wavered at first. He was waiting for the army to contact him about the chaplaincy commission, and he felt a strong sense of responsibility to his church, which was steadily growing under his aggressive leadership. While Billy considered the alternatives facing him, he came down with a serious case of the mumps which rendered him unfit for army duty. The way seemed clear for Billy to join Johnson in Youth for Christ. On May 20, 1944, Billy was scheduled to make his first major appearance for YFC at the Orchestra Hall in Chicago.

Waiting backstage for the meeting to begin Billy

experienced a genuine case of nervousness. He looked through the curtain and saw about three thousand people in the hall, including many men in uniform from Fort Sheridan and the Great Lakes Naval Training Center. At one point Billy didn't know how he could possibly go on stage and preach, but he pulled himself together and tried to forget about the large crowd. When he completed his message forty-two young people came forward to announce decisions for Christ.

The next three years were filled with YFC activities. Billy traveled to scores of towns and cities throughout the United States and Canada, and early in 1947, Graham made his first visit to the British Isles. These were crucial years. Billy gained experience in preaching to large and varied audiences. He also learned administrative skills necessary to put and hold together a large organization. Most important of all, it was during this period that he came into contact with the men who later formed the nucleus of his own evangelistic organization. Cliff Barrows, Billy's longtime songleader and later his television producer and very close friend, joined forces with Billy after meeting him at a North Carolina Bible conference. George Wilson, a brilliant young businessman active in Minneapolis Youth for Christ, became a fast and loyal friend during the meeting in England. During these busy days Billy also added his old Charlotte friends, Grady and T. W. Wilson, to his staff. His services often featured George Beverly Shea, a gifted baritone soloist and recording artist who first met Billy through the "Songs in the Night" radio program.

Those were happy days for Billy. The men worked well together, and Billy gained a reputation as a talented and effective preacher. Through his efforts the Youth for Christ movement was becoming an important force in the evangelical community. These were days of almost non-stop travel. Once Billy narrowly escaped death or serious injury when his plane landed at an Alberta, Canada, airfield in a blizzard. But the landing was only the beginning of his troubles. When Graham arrived at his hotel, he discovered that the storm had filled the hotel with so many persons that he was required to share his room with a stranger. The man was wanted by the police, and in a classic case of mistaken identity, the local law enforcement officials thought Billy was the man they were after. It took a lot of explaining by the pilot and the hotel manager to get Billy out of that jam!

5.

Los Angeles

EARLY IN 1949 Billy received the most important invitation of his career. A group of Los Angeles businessmen asked him to come to their city in September to conduct a series of evangelistic meetings. Billy accepted. He saw this opportunity as a great challenge. Billy had never preached in a city of this size, and he spent the better part of the summer in prayer and Bible study preparing for Los Angeles.

While he appeared calm and natural on the outside, this was a very difficult time for Billy. His preaching reflected great outward confidence and assurance, but he was going through a time of testing, and his very faith seemed at stake. Graham was struggling with the question of the authority of the Scriptures. Was the Bible correct when it claimed that men could be saved through the atoning work of Christ? Some of his friends felt that Billy's faith was too uninformed and childlike, and they raised questions concerning the reliability of the Bible. Billy had already felt a sense of intellectual inadequacy. He had not attended a seminary and his only degree was in liberal arts from Wheaton College. Who was he to stand against professors and authorities who doubted the integrity of the Scripture? His spiritual struggle revolved around one great question. When he called men to accept Christ and offered them the forgiveness of sin and the promise of salvation, was he speaking the truth, or was he leading them astray? At the height of his spiritual crisis Billy was staying at a Christian camp in the San Bernardino mountains near Los Angeles. One night after reading and rereading his Bible, he went for a walk in the mountains. There he arrived at a conclusion made by countless believers, both famous and unknown. He decided to accept the authority of the Bible on faith and not demand rational or intellectual proofs for its trustworthiness. In that moment, alone under the wide California night, Billy girded himself for the Los Angeles meetings and opened the way for his enormously successful ministry. This was a major turning point in his life—what the philosophers like to call a "moment of truth." Never again would doubt over the Bible's authority inhibit his ministry or mar his faith. From that evening on, Billy Graham remained a convicted and convinced servant of God.

Graham left his mountain retreat with renewed

faith and intense determination to succeed in Los Angeles. The three-week crusade, as his city-wide meetings were now called, would provide the most strenuous test yet of his ministry. At thirty-one Graham was still a young man, but he had matured as a Christian, and he felt a great sense of expectancy as his car neared the downtown Los Angeles area where the local committee had erected a huge tent for the crusade. Los Angeles was one of the nation's largest cities. It was famous for its motion picture industry, and each year the city, in magnet-like fashion, drew thousands of young people who hoped to make a career for themselves in the entertainment field. The city was also beginning to experience an influx of people from the South and Midwest who came in search of the area's sunshine and industrial opportunities. Los Angeles also had its share of problems. Its skid row was famous, and behind the glitter of the movie business there was a strong measure of loneliness and alienation as well as disappointment and discouragement faced by many people who failed to crack the film world. Los Angeles was ready for a revival, and Graham sensed the great spiritual void which characterized the city. Almost from the very first service Graham was a success. Thousands of people flocked each night to the tent, and hundreds of people found Christ. The original three-week schedule was extended and then extended again. In all, Graham stayed in Los Angeles for eight weeks. His fame spread throughout California, and through the efforts of the publisher William Randolph Hearst, Graham became a nationally known personality.

Hearst, who controlled a number of big city newspapers, learned of Graham from a maid who worked in his California home. This woman had attended a Graham meeting and told her employer about the evangelist and the work he was doing. Hearst was impressed by this report and sent a two-word message to his editors. The telegram merely said, PUFF GRAHAM, but it was enough to put Billy on the front pages of scores of newspapers. Public awareness of the Los Angeles meetings was also aided by the conversions of three well-known and unlikely candidates for religious expression.

Stuart Hamblen was a local radio-show host, movie actor, and singer. He was a hard-living, hard-drinking Texan who, though brought up in a God-fearing home, had little use for religion. One night he and his wife, Suzy, attended the crusade. Hamblen went to jeer, but he found the message interesting, yet uncomfortable. The Hamblens went back on other nights, and then after Stuart began to struggle with the possibility of accepting Christ, he called Graham at two o'clock one morning and asked to see him. He and Suzy went over to the apartment where Billy and Ruth were staying. Once there they were joined by Grady Wilson. After much prayer and straight talk from Billy, who told Stuart to stop fooling around and come to a decision, the cowboy star gave in and asked Christ to come into his life.

Later that day Hamblen announced his conversion

on his popular radio show, and the news caused a sensation. The Hamblen episode was followed by the conversion of Jim Vaus, an ex-convict with close connections to the underworld. Vaus took his wife to a Sunday afternoon meeting more out of curiosity than anything else. He was even then making final plans to leave for the Midwest for the most important criminal episode of his career, but Graham's preaching reached him, and he and his wife responded to the invitation and received Christ. The news of Vaus's conversion added momentum to the press interest aroused by Stuart Hamblen. The conversion of Louis Zamperini, a star athlete on the 1936 U.S. Olympic team, followed. By the time Graham left Los Angeles he was exhausted, but he had made his mark as an evangelist of imposing stature.

6.

The Hour of Decision

THE TWO MEN SAT CONTENTEDLY in front of a roaring fire. They were old friends, and their conversation took in some of the world's most famous names. One of the men, Bernard Baruch, was a self-made millionaire who rose from poverty to become an adviser to several presidents. The other man, Henry Luce, founded *Time* magazine and created a publishing empire. Now, as they rested in the comfortable setting of Baruch's South Carolina estate, their talk turned to a young evangelist who was then holding a crusade in the nearby city of Columbia. Luce, who had read press accounts of the Los Angeles tent sessions, expressed a keen interest in meeting the well-known preacher. Baruch promptly called the auditorium in Columbia and invited Billy Graham to his home. The next night Billy spent several hours in discussion with Luce. This was to prove a most important meeting, for Luce became a supporter of his work, and from that time on, the Luce publications often featured stories about the evangelist and his activities.

Graham followed up the Los Angeles sessions with outstanding meetings in New England and the South, and by the early 1950s he had a national following. He also had a nationwide radio audience which heard him each Sunday evening on a half-hour program called "The Hour of Decision." "The Hour of Decision" broadcast was the foundation stone of Billy's later success. This program put him in touch with countless numbers of people who could not attend his meetings, and their gifts and encouragement enabled Graham to expand his ministry. The radio show had a rather humble origin. In the summer of 1950 Billy was holding a crusade in Portland, Oregon. He was visited there by two energetic advertising men who were partners in a small Chicago-based firm. Fred Dienert and Walter Bennett urged Graham to consider the possibility of a weekly, half-hour nationwide radio program. Graham was busy with the Portland meetings, and he couldn't see how the funds for the show, $25,000 for the first thirteen weeks, could be raised. Dienert and Bennett continued to try to convince Graham, and at one point Billy was so pestered by them that he fled to nearby Mt. Hood on his day off. Finally the two partners involved Billy in serious consideration of the project. Graham, who believed in testing a project by faith, said, "All right, we will do it if the $25,000 can be raised in one night after I mention the need to the crusade audience." That night Billy told of the great radio opportunity which awaited him if the necessary money could be raised. He asked those interested in contributing to come to the platform after the service where he would accept their pledges. Once the service had ended a long line of people gathered to give and pledge sums ranging from two thousand dollars to one dollar. Billy and his associates went to dinner while the crusade chairman counted the collection. He met Graham in the restaurant and reported that $23,000 had been raised. While the sum amazed him, Billy said that this was not enough, and apparently the radio idea was dead. At fifteen minutes to midnight Grady Wilson checked his mail in the hotel and was handed three envelopes containing pledges for the remaining two thousand dollars. The test of faith was met, and within a matter of weeks "The Hour of Decision," so named by Ruth Graham, went on the air.

The program was an immediate success, and Graham was faced with an avalanche of mail from listeners. This response caused Graham to set up a formal organization known as the Billy Graham Evangelistic Association. This body became the channel for contributions to his work and would later be recognized as one of the most efficient religious organizations in the world. Graham asked his Minneapolis friend, George Wilson, to head the Association. This proved to be a good choice. Wilson was familiar with sound business practice, and he proceeded to build a smooth-running organization. The Association was also important because it gave Graham credibility as a man of high integrity and purpose. In earlier times evangelists were often criticized for the manner in which they handled funds, and for some people the very word *evangelist* had negative connotations. Graham, by establishing a formal structure to handle the increasingly large funds which supported his work, helped to put evangelism on a firmer footing and gave the calling much needed respectability. Today, Billy is paid a salary similar to that of a middle-level executive in a large corporation, and his Association very carefully accounts for all income and expenditures.

7.

The London Crusade

THE DAY WAS BLEAK AND GRAY. The rain and fog
covered the city with a depressing dampness, and
the fact that it was Sunday added little cheer to the
overall atmosphere. The intense chill seemed to pen-
etrate the walls of the old church in London's West
End as the Rev. Arthur Williams mounted the pulpit to begin his sermon. As Rev. Williams looked
out at his audience, he was dispirited. The church,
once a center of neighborhood activity and worship,
was less than one quarter filled. When the service
ended, Rev. Williams, instead of greeting his parishioners at the church door, returned to his study.
There he fell to his knees and prayed for a spiritual
revival to sweep the city and nation he loved. Unknown to him, clergymen throughout the British
Isles were uttering similar petitions. It was out of

this deeply felt need that some months later an invitation would be extended to a young American evangelist, asking him to cross the ocean and spark a fire in England's hungry soul.

In the early 1950s while Billy was busy establishing his Association and holding crusades in a number of American cities, his activities were being watched with keen interest overseas. In England, a group of church and community leaders greatly troubled by declining church attendance in their country followed Graham's activities with special interest. In 1953 they decided to invite the evangelist and his team to London for a crusade to open on March 1, 1954. This crusade was Graham's greatest opportunity and greatest challenge to date.

England was still struggling with the aftereffects of World War II. Her church people were apathetic; her national life was riddled with secularism. The question was whether Graham could light a fire under the British churches. To some, Graham, with his southern accent and rapid fire delivery, did not seem well-suited to the more formal atmosphere of England, and there were predictions of his failure on both sides of the Atlantic.

In England Graham received a hostile reception from both the weather and, more importantly, the press. It was cold and damp, and the Americans found it difficult to adjust to the poorly-heated London hotels and meeting rooms. The press seemed to be out for the evangelist's blood. He was pictured as heading a three-ring circus which would flop the

minute Londoners caught on to his act. It is understandable, then, that Billy was nervous on the evening of March 1 as he waited in his hotel room for
the car to take him and Ruth to Harringay Arena,
the site of the meetings. The cold and the steadily
falling sleet did nothing to improve his mood. Just
before Billy left his hotel an aide called from Harringay to say that the arena was less than half filled.
With this disquieting news the Grahams, holding
hands and silently praying, drove out to Harringay.
When they reached the arena a member of the team
came running up to their car to tell them that the
hall was filled and that hundreds were being turned
away.

For the next twelve weeks, despite some of the
worst spring weather on record and the continuing
hostility of the London press, Graham filled the
arena night after night. Thousands of people made
decisions for Christ. The news of the London triumph reached back to America and made Billy a
household name. The crusade ended on May 22
with two great rallies: one in the afternoon at White
City Stadium where 60,000 people gathered in pour-
ing rain, and the other that evening at the famous
Wembley Football Stadium where 120,000 people,
the largest crowd in the history of the British Isles
to that time, met to say farewell to the American
evangelist. So great was the traffic and crush on the
roads surrounding the field that Graham and his
team almost didn't get to Wembley on time.

At the conclusion of the service, Grady Wilson,

the gregarious Southern boy, and Dr. Geoffrey Fisher, the austere Archbishop of Canterbury, embraced, and thousands of other people were caught up in a spirit of comradeship and joy. A few days later Graham was escorted into the office of one of the twentieth century's most famous men, Winston Churchill, then prime minister of England. Billy told the aging leader that Christ was the only answer to world problems, and the Prime Minister, not generally known for spending time with clergymen, seemed greatly affected by the American evangelist. Later Churchill told his secretary that he had been greatly impressed by Graham.

Almost 40,000 people had made decisions for Christ during the London Crusade. This was an amazing response, particularly in the light of the early severe press criticism and the reservations many British clergy harbored about Graham and his methods.

When the great Wembley Stadium meeting ended, Graham was physically exhausted. His intuition told him to continue, to tour the British Isles with his team and continue the momentum of the London meetings. He sensed that Great Britain was on the threshold of a great spiritual revival. However, perhaps because of fatigue, counsel from advisers, or misjudgment, Graham decided to go ahead with his scheduled visits to continental Europe and his commitment to hold crusades in Nashville, Tennessee, and New Orleans. Later he looked back upon this decision as ill-considered. This episode was remark-

ably similar to an incident which took place early
in 1950 in New England.

At that time Billy was riding the crest of excite-
ment created by the Los Angeles crusade and experiencing great success in Boston and several other
New England cities. New England had long been
recognized as the seat of theological liberalism. Evangelicals had always found it difficult to maintain a
solid base of operations in the region, and when
Graham went to Boston in January of 1950, many
thought he would fail completely. What actually happened was a great response, with the famous Boston
Garden hockey rink filled to capacity night after
night. At the height of the Boston rallies Billy was
scheduled to travel to Toronto and then to fly on to
Columbia, South Carolina, for a long-planned crusade. As his train sped across Massachusetts, he felt
a strong force leading him back to Boston. Twice,
at Worcester and at Springfield, he almost left the
train. In the end he decided that his schedule must
take precedence over his intuition, and he continued
on to Canada and then to South Carolina. Later
Billy said that he had innocently "disobeyed the
voice of God." These incidents point up the difficulties Graham faced as his organization developed and
his fame increased. He became a victim of his success. He could not improve or suddenly change his
schedule, which by the end of the 1950s was set
several years in advance. He was, as in the case of
New England and Great Britain, often faced with
the question of breaking his schedule in order to re-

main in an area where he was experiencing particular success. His pattern was to disregard the inner compulsions to stay put and to go through with prearranged programs. A less important man could juggle dates and appointments. Graham, obviously, felt a strong sense of responsibility to the committees in various cities who spent months and even years preparing for crusades.

Graham visited Scotland, Scandinavia, Germany, and Canada in 1955, and the following January he spoke to over 800,000 people in an eight-week crusade in India. That year he also held meetings in Richmond, Virginia; Oklahoma City; and Louisville, Kentucky. Then in the spring of 1957 Graham faced the most difficult challenge of his career—a crusade in New York's Madison Square Garden. This was the first crusade Graham ever held in an area not predominantly Protestant.

8.

Appointment at Madison Square Garden

"THEY SAY NEVER ARGUE politics or religion, but lately in this cab all I hear people talk about is religion." As the driver said this, his taxicab almost smashed into a car parked in front of Madison Square Garden. His passenger drew in a quick breath, then reached into his pocket to pay the fare. The driver turned around, looked at the man and exclaimed, "Hey buddy, you're Billy Graham!" The evangelist nodded his head and asked the driver if he was going to the crusade. "Well, I have to work another six hours, and anyway, I haven't been to church in twenty years." The passenger persisted and handed the driver a ticket to the reserved-seat section of the Garden. "Come on your day off," he said. "I'll be looking for you." The driver then did something very unusual for a New York cabby—he was speechless. Suddenly he took Graham's hand and said, "That's the first time in years that anyone showed an interest in me. I'm really grateful, and I will come to hear you on my next night off!" The evangelist left the cab and silently prayed for the driver who by now had steered his car back into the rush of the Eighth Avenue traffic.

New York was a melting pot of many religious and ethnic groups. In addition, the city was known for its sophistication and culture, and many wondered if New Yorkers could possibly relate to Graham's Southern speech and evangelistic techniques. Graham spent weeks getting ready for the New York meetings. He realized that the eyes of the nation and the world would be on him, and he was determined to preach an effective soul-winning message. New York was the capital of the communications industry. The three major television networks, the top news magazines, and the highly influential and nationally circulated *New York Times* were headquartered in America's largest city. Whatever happened at the Garden, whether good or bad, would be immediately transmitted over the press wires and airwaves.

Even before the crusade opened on the evening of May 15, Graham was the center of a swirl of controversy. Many of his supporters and advisers thought he was being reckless to attempt a crusade in New York—a city viewed by many believers as beyond the hope of redemption. Liberal Christians were upset by the invitation extended by the local Council of Churches and criticized Graham for what they felt was undue stress on personal salvation at the expense of social reform. Ardent fundamentalists, such as Bob Jones, attacked Graham for joining forces with the Council of Churches. A lesser man would have turned tail and canceled the crusade, but Graham was by this time used to criticism from both the theological left and right, and he believed the Spirit of God was leading him to New York. He also realized the psychological gain he would make if he were successful in the Garden Crusade. News of a spiritual awakening in New York would stun the rest of the country and have wide impact in many other nations. Victory in New York City could start a chain reaction which might reverberate around the world.

Graham went to New York with tremendous confidence that he was doing the will of God. He believed that God was about to perform a great work among the city's restless millions. A notation in his diary in the days just before his departure for the huge metropolis gives insight into his frame of mind. "I am convinced that the Holy Spirit is going to answer the prayers of millions. My desk has been flooded daily with letters from all over the world informing me of the thrilling experiences that Christians are having everywhere praying for the New York crusade. I have received letters from over forty-five countries, some of them unbelievable letters of people praying many times all night that God would send a spiritual awakening to New York City. I believe that in his own way God will answer those multiple prayers."

In all Graham stayed in the Garden for sixteen weeks and preached to a total of 2,400,000 persons, including a packed rally at Yankee Stadium. Over sixty-one thousand people made decisions for Christ, and thousands more became involved in the activity of New York area churches. During the crusade Graham went into several New York neighborhoods, and on one memorable occasion conducted a meeting in Manhattan's heavily black Harlem district. The Harlem rally, sponsored by the Heart of Harlem Neighborhood Association of the Protestant Council, was scheduled for outdoors, but a sudden rainstorm forced the meeting into Salem Methodist Church located on the strategic corner of 129th Street and Seventh Avenue. On the afternoon of the meeting Billy left his midtown hotel in a taxi with Howard Jones, a young black minister who had taken temporary leave from his Cleveland congregation to work with Graham at the Garden. Jones first met Graham when he had come out of curiosity to one of the first New York sessions and later asked to speak to the evangelist. Billy was struck by Jones's confident manner and great sense of mission, and the two men became fast friends. On the way uptown to Harlem Billy expressed fears that few people would come to hear him. But Jones, who had talked with black pastors and had a finger on the pulse of the black community, assured him that attendance would be good. When the rainstorm broke Billy went into a period of gloom, but Howard kept predicting that all would go well. Jones was entirely correct. When Graham stepped from the cab, people in nearby houses shouted greetings. He entered a packed church. His message was received with great interest and enthusiasm, and Jones believes the Harlem appearance was a factor in a significant black attendance throughout the remainder of the crusade.

One of the New York Crusade's most dramatic moments came when Ethel Waters, a famous entertainer who had, unknown to Graham, sat with the choir night after night, was recognized by Cliff Barrows and asked to come to the microphone for a solo. Miss Waters, who had a strong religious upbringing, but had experienced more than her share of troubles and heartache in her long and illustrious career, sang *Nobody Knows the Trouble I've Seen* and the song she made famous on Broadway, *His Eye Is on the Sparrow*. Ever since New York, Ethel has, at her own expense, traveled to many U.S. crusades, and she is a most welcome platform addition to the Graham program. At the end of the crusade Dr. Dan Potter, executive secretary of the New York City Council of Churches, wrote that the crusade had reached its four objectives of winning persons to Christ; making New York God-conscious; strengthening the churches; and making the city aware of her moral, spiritual, and social responsibilities.

Billy Graham saw the crusade as changing thousands of lives in New York, and he urged the local churches to work with those persons who had come

forward to receive Christ. Graham also used the New
York Crusade to launch another important aspect of
his ministry—national television. This was the first
of his crusades to be shown on television, and the
audience response was amazing. On June 1 he
preached to a packed Garden and to six to seven
million people watching in their homes. The weekly
news magazine, *Time,* graphically described this first
telecast: "The long arms chopped the smokeless air
of Manhattan's Madison Square Garden and the fore-
finger jabbed at the TV screen. Right in your living
room came the muscular Southern voice, right in
your bedrooms, right in a bar, you can let Christ
come in. Wearing TV blue but no make-up, Caro-
lina-tanned Billy Graham was bringing down the
third act curtain on the first live U.S. telecast of his
New York Crusade." As a result of this telecast thousands of letters poured into the Association's Minneapolis office, and Graham was convinced of the great
value of television exposure. From this point on,
television would be an important part of his crusade
operations.

9.

To the Land Down Under

IN THE SPRING OF 1959 Billy Graham made his longest journey up to that time. He and his team flew to Australia for a series of meetings, which was indeed a long way for the North Carolina–born evengelist to travel. Billy and his associates had to do a considerable amount of studying about the people and culture of that vast continent preparing for their visit. The very size of Australia was a great challenge to Graham, who was used to preaching in individual cities or countries. Even his tours of the British Isles were undertaken in a relatively small geographical area. Now, however, Billy would have to hopscotch across the length and breadth of "the land down under" to reach as many Australians as possible with his message. Graham was greatly aided by Jerry Beaven in his Australian efforts. Beaven, who was assigned responsibility to direct the Australian Crusade, and his family went to Sydney in the spring of 1958 to make preparations for Graham's visit. Beaven had joined Graham in 1950 for the Boston Garden rallies. Before that Jerry had worked as the registrar of Northwestern Bible School and when he learned that Graham was going to Boston, he asked Billy if he could come along to help. From that time on, Beaven served as Graham's press secretary and later took on important special assignments.

Another of Graham's associates who was extremely helpful in setting up the Australian sessions was Walter Smyth, an old friend and associate of Billy's who had first met the evangelist during his days at Wheaton and had later worked with him in Youth for Christ.

From the opening session in Melbourne the crusade was a tremendous success. Grady Wilson wrote a friend in Florida, "We are seeing God do a mighty thing here in Australia." The days in Australia were filled with meetings, prayer, and a renewed dedication which molded the Graham team into a close-knit unit. On the last day of the crusade, over 130,000 people came to the Melbourne Cricket Ground, and 4,000 people came forward when Graham gave the invitation. From Melbourne Graham went on to Sydney, another major Australian city, and on the last day of the Sydney Crusade even more people turned out than had at Melbourne. The Australian tour of 1959 climaxed an action-packed and event-filled decade for Graham. During the last ten years Graham had traveled to almost every major world area. He had delivered countless sermons and had seen tens of thousands of people respond to the offer to receive Christ. The ten years between the end of the Los Angeles Crusade and the Australia tour were also a time of solidification and growth for Graham's Evangelistic Association. It was during this decade that the Association had been incorporated, that the "Hour of Decision" radio program had been born, and that Graham had first employed national television as an evangelistic tool. During the 1950s he had become a world-renowned personality and his London and New York Crusades had established him as the foremost evangelist of the era.

10.

Major Crusade of the Sixties

THE 1960s SEEMED TO HOLD great promise for a continuation of Billy's crusade efforts, and he held a series of crusades in many of the world's largest and most important cities. At the same time, during the 1960s, the United States witnessed great domestic turmoil, and Graham spent time wrestling with the problems of race, poverty, and American involvement in overseas conflicts. During this period Graham became the major spokesman for the world's evangelical Christians, and his statements and comments on a wide range of issues were eagerly read by millions of his followers, as well as by those who were unfriendly to his work and views.

Graham's important crusades in the 1960s included Philadelphia, New York City, Los Angeles, and London. In the fall of 1961 Graham conducted a month long crusade in the nation's third largest city, Philadelphia. The Greater Philadelphia Crusade had an attendance of 630,000, and over 16,000 people made decisions for Christ. This was the largest number of decisions in any of Graham's one month crusades in the United States. In fact, the final day's attendance of 83,000 was his single largest U.S. audience, with the exception of the 100,000 who jammed Yankee Stadium during the New York Crusade in 1957. Graham also used the crusade for national television programming, and eight of the twenty-six meetings were videotaped. On the opening night 25,000 gathered in an outdoor stadium despite thunder, lightning, and heavy rain. Just before the meeting was to start Billy and Grady Wilson wondered if the crowd would remain for the entire service. At one point, Billy looked out at the lightning flashing over the stadium and remarked that it would be a miracle if anyone was left in the stands when it was time for the sermon to begin. Grady and Billy then fell to their knees in prayer asking that the rain stop so the meeting could function smoothly. The rain, instead of stopping, only increased in intensity as the service progressed, and when Billy got up from his seat on the platform to go to the podium, a savage bolt of lightning crackled over the center of the field. Incredibly enough, no one in the stadium left during the sermon, and later Billy told the team, "This is the first time an American audience of such a size has remained in the rain for a sermon, or for any kind of an event."

The weather really seemed to be at odds with the Philadelphia Crusade. On the first Sunday the temperature reached 96 degrees, and the humidity in the stadium was stifling. Despite these uncomfortable conditions, over 60,000 people came out to hear Graham preach. At the conclusion of the Crusade several Philadelphia-area church leaders commented favorably upon the impact the meetings had made. The local Methodist bishop, Dr. Fred Corson, said that the crusade "lived up to the best expectations of those who urged Dr. Graham to come." He added, "The campaign committed the Christian forces of the Greater Philadelphia area in a healthy, constructive way. It was a dramatic mass witness for public decency and personal righteousness. It has created a climate in which it is easy to speak about religion. The church must take the initiative to follow up."

In September of 1963 Graham returned to Los Angeles, the scene of his first great success. He remained in Southern California for twenty-five days and preached to over 930,000 people. On the last day of the crusade 134,254 made their way through the turnstiles of the famous Memorial Coliseum. In his sermon Graham, referring to the big crowd, said, "We have enough people here to march on Washington, and if they keep throwing the Bible out of the schools we might just do that." Graham was alluding to the great "March on Washington for Jobs and Freedom" which had occurred only a few weeks before. During the Los Angeles sessions Graham announced that he was suspending his overseas travels in order to concentrate on the American situation for the next two years. He told his audience, "In my opinion the next twenty-four months will decide the destiny of the United States."

This crusade in California's largest city contrasted sharply with the Graham crusade conducted fourteen years before in 1949. At that time Graham was a relatively unknown thirty-one-year-old minister and Youth for Christ representative. The crusade itself was held in a tent in the downtown area, and a good number of the local churches refused to support the evangelist's visit. During the first Los Angeles Crusade Graham's preaching consisted almost entirely of the "old time religion," focusing heavily on sin and salvation. In 1963, Graham had the support of the great majority of local area churches. He preached in the huge coliseum, and his message had more timeliness. He stressed personal salvation and man's need to find Christ, but his messages also described the turmoil of contemporary American life and solutions for the nation's problems. A visitor to both crusades might have noticed a maturing in Graham's delivery. He was much less dramatic and his sermons appeared to be rather low-key. In 1963 Graham did not need spectacular conversions to excite the community and increase attendance. He was already an established Christian leader, and people appeared to be more interested in what he had to say than in the response of well-known individuals to his message. At the end of the crusade Graham told a reporter for the *New York Times,* "I think there's probably a deeper interest in genuine religious experience on a personal level than ever before. I think there's been some disenchantment and disillusionment with organized churches. But more and more people are tending to meet in small groups. Today the greatest response I've had is on college campuses. I have hundreds of invitations to speak there. Ten years ago they wouldn't have had me."

11.

Return Visits to
New York and London

BY THE END of the second Los Angeles crusade, Billy
Graham had reconfirmed his standing as the greatest
evangelist of the age. He was still, however, a humble
person. Before he left Los Angeles he said, "I am
what every evangelist has been, the herald, the
trumpeter, telling the good news of the gospel. I can't
convert anybody. God converts them. I am only the
channel through which he works."

During the mid-1960s Graham returned to England for a month-long crusade in London. In addition, Billy visited several English cities, appeared
on television, and preached at both Cambridge and
Oxford universities. One night during the London
Crusade Billy, wearing dark glasses and a hunting
cap, traveled with several associates and local committee members to the city's Soho district. This area

was known for rowdy activities and was a meeting place for those interested in worldly entertainments. Billy wanted to invite some of the area's residents to his Earls Court meetings. He was also intent on witnessing to the individuals who spent their time in the neighborhood's bars. This was not a new strategy for Graham. Years before when a student of Florida Bible Institute, he had walked into a Tampa saloon quoting Bible verses. The bartender on duty promptly threw Billy out the door. On this particular night in Soho Billy stood on the roof of an automobile and preached a brief sermon. He also mingled with the crowds and had the opportunity to discuss his faith with several interested persons.

In June 1969, Graham returned to New York for a ten-night crusade at the new Madison Square Garden. This arena was located about a mile south of the site of Graham's famous 1957 sixteen-week crusade. A day before the crusade opened Graham told the press that he had come to New York for three reasons: "To win individuals to a personal experience with Christ, because I believe it is possible to have a personal experience with God; to make a commitment to the renewal of spiritual life church leaders in New York have been urging, and to emphasize the social responsibilities Christians have on local and national levels." Graham added that his sermons would include material on poverty, race, and war. He also put special stress on reaching the city's young people. Each night after the Madison Square Garden service, a coffee house, complete

with rock music and psychedelic lights, was operated at the nearby Manhattan Center. The coffee
house was the first such experiment of its kind for
the Graham Association. Graham also told a large
group of reporters that one only had to walk through
the Times Square area to understand why another
crusade in New York City was a necessity. He was
especially troubled by the area's many pornography
shops and by the wave of sex and nudity which
seemed to be highly fashionable in New York's
movies and legitimate theater. One day during the
week before the crusade started, Graham wanted to
take his youngest son to a movie, but after spending
several minutes reading the amusement page of the
local newspaper, he threw up his arms in disgust at
not being able to find one film he thought suitable
for family viewing.

Graham filled the Garden every night, and millions
watched the proceedings on television in twelve
East-Coast cities. About a thousand people came
forward each evening in response to the invitation
to receive Christ. The inquirers, as they are called
in the Graham organization, included a cross-section
of New York area residents.

In his preaching Graham seemed particularly con-
cerned with the afterlife and Christ's second coming.
He told his audience, "I don't think anyone knows
how to live unless he knows how to die." He added,
"God commands all men everywhere to repent.
Nothing else counts in this life and the life to come

unless you have obeyed that one great command-
ment: 'Repent!' "

On the last night of the crusade he predicted that
Christ would return again "not as the Babe of
Bethlehem, but as King of the world." He expressed
his belief that the second coming of Christ could
occur soon. As always, Graham's preaching was
highly topical; he made constant references to social
problems and situations of current interest within
the society. One night he preached on the verse
"Narrow is the path that leads to salvation." He
remarked, "The Bible says the road to heaven is
through a narrow gate and a narrow road and we
don't like to be narrow. We think of ourselves as
broadminded and tolerant. Suppose the Apollo 11
astronauts going to the moon in July have a navi-
gator at the control center in Houston who's broadminded and tolerant. The astronauts say, 'Well,
we're way off course.' 'Oh,' he says, 'it's all right.
There are many roads that lead to the moon. Just
take the one you're on.' Well, they would be just as
wrong as the people who claim there are many roads
that lead to salvation."

12.

Television as an Evangelistic Tool

A PLEASANT, CLEAR-FACED YOUNG MAN moved swiftly and efficiently through the large trailer. He studied a series of dials and controls and from time to time softly uttered instructions to the technicians seated nearby. Ted Dienert, the son of long-time Graham adviser Fred Dienert and a son-in-law of the evangelist, was in his favorite working environment, the mini-studio controlling the taping of a crusade meeting. Dienert is the producer responsible for the Graham television programs and this show would ultimately be seen by millions of people around the world. As he worked, Ted exemplified the team spirit which characterizes the activities of the Billy Graham Evangelistic Association.

In the 1970s Graham continued his world travels, although he reduced his crusade schedule. Beginning in the early 1970s the Graham organization adopted a new strategy related to the evangelist's schedule. A much greater stress was placed on television and Graham appeared in medium-sized cities such as Albuquerque, New Mexico; Lubbock, Texas; and Jackson, Mississippi, where a crusade was relatively easy to organize, and the crusade site became a large television studio.

At Albuquerque, for example, Graham preached in a 15,000 seat arena, and several sessions were taped for later television broadcasts. Although Graham was not spending as much time in any one city as he had in the past—for instance his 1975 Jackson Crusade lasted ten days, whereas twenty-three years before he had spent four weeks in the Mississippi capital—he was working just as hard, or harder, on each individual series of meetings. Television made great physical and mental demands on the evangelist. When he stood up to preach with the television cameras turned on, he realized that what he was saying in a specific American city would be heard later throughout the world. While he was talking to the residents of a west Texas town, he would have to be thinking of what his message would mean to people in Africa, India, on the European continent, and in the islands of the Pacific. The strains created by television caused Graham to spend much time studying during the actual course of a crusade. On the day that a crusade session is to be taped he works hard memorizing his sermon. This usually occupies four to six hours of his time. He likes to look directly into the camera and not refer to notes or to a typed script of his message. At the Jackson Crusade, he virtually isolated himself for five of the ten days in his room at the Holiday Inn North, which was filled with study aids, books, and file cards filled with sermon material. During this type of crusade Graham's staff is responsible for meeting with the scores of people who would like to see Graham personally. These associates are occupied from early morning until late evening with many of the details, while Billy concentrates on the message he will try to preach.

Part Two

*Billy Graham and
Major Issues*

13.

The Vietnam War

THE TWO MEN HAD JUST FINISHED a round of golf under the warm Florida sun. Neither man excelled at the game, but they found the sport to be a welcome diversion from the pressure of everyday business. Both were famous and immediately recognizable, and in a few days one of them was to be inaugurated President of the United States. When they got to the clubhouse at the Seminole Club, John F. Kennedy began to tell Billy Graham about several of the domestic and international problems that faced him as he prepared to assume office. While Mr. Kennedy's most immediate problem was Cuba, he also mentioned a far-away area called Indochina. He looked worried when he discussed this region and closed the conversation by saying, "Billy, we simply cannot allow South Vietnam to fall to the Communists."

This was the first time the evangelist learned that the United States might become involved in an Asian land war. Billy Graham and the rest of America were to hear much more about Vietnam before the decade closed.

Graham has always been a keen student of current affairs. He follows the news very carefully and is especially interested in events taking place outside of the United States. Over the years he has preached the gospel on every continent and in almost every major city. He is very conscious of his international following, and in his sermons, books, and public statements he tries to communicate with people of many different national backgrounds. He is a firm believer in the Great Commission of Matthew 28, and throughout the years of his ministry he and his associates have gone out into the world to preach the gospel. In attempting to communicate with people outside the United States, Graham has consistently taken the position that he is an ambassador for Christ rather than a representative for America. He has tried to steer clear of the error some evangelicals have made in the past of equating patriotism with Christianity. Graham is a dedicated citizen with great love for his native land. He does feel, however, that he serves a higher power. His ultimate allegiance is to the kingdom of God rather than to a given state or nation. Billy has kept many evangelicals from making a religion of Americanism.

Even today there are preachers and church people who believe that the American way of life is equal to the way of Christ's kingdom. Contemporary life styles in the United States show clearly how far off the mark this philosophy is. During the course of his career Graham has tried to avoid controversial international issues, but he does have personal views. At times he has commented on some of the more troubling problems in the international sphere.

During the middle and late 1960s the United States was divided over the war. Graham believed the division could make the North Vietnamese believe that they would ultimately triumph. He went so far as to say that the protestors against the war "were giving comfort to the enemy."

The infamous My Lai incident in which American troups massacred a number of Vietnamese civilians provoked Graham's most comprehensive statement on the war. On April 9, 1971, the evangelist published an article in the *New York Times* concerning the trial of Lt. William L. Calley, Jr., the young officer in charge of the American troops at My Lai. Graham stated that the first time he had realized the United States might become involved in Indochina was on January 28, 1961. In commenting specifically on the My Lai episode Graham stated, "We're learning one thing—that Sherman was right, war is hell. I have never heard of a war where innocent people were not killed. Tens of thousands of innocent people were killed at Hiroshima and Nagasaki. I have been to Vietnam several times, and I have heard some of the most horrible stories from missionaries and Vietnamese people about sadistic murders by the Viet Cong of innocent people. I talked to men who will never walk again who are suffering from booby-trap or grenade wounds planted or thrown by women and children working for the Viet Cong."

14.

The Holy Land

THE EVIDENCE OF A CONTINUING BATTLE with food poisoning was etched on the evangelist's face. Billy Graham, accompanied by his associates, Grady Wilson and Walter Smyth, had just arrived in Israel after suffering the sudden illness while on a visit to Cairo, Egypt. Now seated on a couch in the VIP lounge of Ben Gurion International Airport, Graham patiently answered reporters' questions and taped an interview for Israeli radio. Finally an official of the Foreign Ministry handed Billy his passport and ushered him to a waiting limousine. Graham stepped into the warm sunshine of a late November Tel Aviv day, and his spirits rose. This was his first trip to Israel in several years, and he looked forward to seeing what new additions had been made to the developing Jewish state. As he was about to enter the automobile, a group of Christian pilgrims from Holland spotted him and walked over to greet Graham. One of the Foreign Ministry representatives commented, "It is so pleasant to have Billy in Israel, we feel he understands us and identifies with our national life."

The other world area which has preoccupied Graham over the entire course of his public ministry has been the Middle East. Evangelicals take a keen interest in that region of the world because they believe that many of the final events of history will occur there. One of the most important points in evangelical teaching concerns the restoration of the Jewish people to their ancient homeland. When the State of Israel was declared on May 14, 1948, many evangelicals saw this event as a significant confirmation of their faith. They believed that the creation of Israel was a fulfillment of prophecies contained in many portions of the Old Testament. In the Book of Ezekiel, chapter 37, the prophet describes the valley of dry bones and the future time when these bones will be molded together again. Then the Jewish people will return to their land from all parts of the world. It is, therefore, understandable that evangelicals follow events in Israel very closely, and Graham is no exception. He has visited Israel many times and some of that nation's political leaders are numbered among his close friends. In 1970 World Wide Pictures, the Graham organization's film subsidiary, released a stirring hour-long production filmed on location in Israel and entitled *His*

Land. The film, which shows the reality and dynamism of modern Israel, relates Bible prophecy to the restoration of the Jewish state. Within a two-year period over 10,000,000 people viewed the film, and it remains one of the all-time favorites in the Graham film library. In 1975 Graham visited Israel and spent a whole day inspecting sites of religious interest in Jerusalem. At the end of the day Graham visited the Hadassah Hospital where several people wounded just the week before in a terrorist bombing lay recovering. Graham walked up and down the ward stopping at each bed to give a word of cheer and support. At the end of the room one bed was surrounded by medical equipment and devices which monitored the condition of a man hurt very critically by the blast. The man could not speak, but after Billy whispered something in his ear, he looked at the evangelist and, using up most of his available strength, moved his lips in a silent thank you. Tears welled in the evangelist's eyes as he and his associates left the hospital. A few days after Graham's visit to the Holy Land, Prime Minister Yitzhak Rabin told an aide, "Billy Graham is one of the world's finest gentlemen. He has been a true friend of Israel and he is always welcome in our country. There is simply no question but that evangelical Christians have been our staunchest American supporters in our struggle to exist as a free and independent nation."

Graham has also been received by the heads of state of scores of nations. Foreign leaders often seek his advice and counsel, and many of these dignitaries believe Graham can make a great impact for good in their lands.

Billy is, of course, also intensely interested in happenings within the United States. He often joins with other Americans in promoting stability and moral values. On one such occasion he participated in an event calling Americans back to their noble heritage.

15.

Honor America Day

IT WAS VERY HUMID, as summer afternoons in the nation's capital tend to be. Inside the air-conditioned comfort of the Crystal City Marriott Hotel, George Wilson, the buoyant vice-president of the Billy Graham Evangelistic Association, was greeting a number of celebrities who had traveled from all over the country to join with Billy in Washington, D.C. to celebrate the Fourth of July. As George was talking with an associate, a loud murmur swept through the lobby, and he looked up to see famed entertainer Bob Hope coming through the entrance. "Gosh, Bob," George said, "it's really great to have you here, and I know Billy is very anxious to see you." "Well, I hope so," cracked Bob, "especially if Billy's speech tomorrow is better than his golf score last time we played together out in California."

Bob Hope was referring to a major talk the evangelist would give the next morning at the Lincoln Memorial.

July 4 arrived in traditional fashion. By 10:00 A.M., the temperature was already in the low 90s; the sky was blue, and the sound of marching bands could be heard all over the grounds adjacent to the Lincoln Memorial. At 11:00 A.M. a religious service was held before 5,000 persons seated in front of the Memorial and a nationwide television audience. The service was part of a day-long celebration known as Honor America Day. The festivities had been planned by a group of political leaders working with leading personalities from the worlds of the media, entertainment, and religion. The object of Honor America Day was to try to get people together to proclaim their belief in America and its institutions. The celebration emerged from a conversation Billy Graham had had with Hobart D. Lewis, president and editor-in-chief of *Reader's Digest*. Lewis and Graham enlisted the support of former Presidents Lyndon B. Johnson and Harry S. Truman, and the chairmen of both the Republican and Democratic National Committees. Another co-sponsor of the event and a participant in the evening entertainment portion of the Honor America Day program was comedian Bob Hope. Billy Graham was the featured speaker at the religious service and was joined by Jewish and Roman Catholic clergymen, as well as by Kate Smith, who favored the crowd with her breathtaking performance of "God Bless America."

As Billy stood up to preach, a large group of young people shouting anti–Vietnam War slogans began to make their way through the wading pool which separates the Lincoln Memorial from the Washington Monument. At times they threatened to drown out Graham, but the louder they shouted, the more determined the evangelist was to get his message across. His speech on July 4, 1970, was entitled "The Unfinished Democracy," and was based on 1 Peter 2:17. Graham interpreted that verse to mean "honor the nation," and he began by saying, "Today in the capital of the United States thousands of us have come together to honor America on her 194th birthday." Graham added, "We are not only here today to honor America, but we have come as citizens to renew our dedication and allegiance to the principles and institutions that made her great." Graham asked his audience to "pursue a new vision under God, to work for freedom and for peace, to labor relentlessly, to serve selflessly, to pray earnestly, and to die nobly if need be. It will not be easy. The journey will be hard. The day will be long. The obstacles will be many."

Just as the shouts of the young people in the wading pool were the loudest, Graham told of the time Sir Winston Churchill returned to his prep school to give the graduation address. The former prime minister rose to his feet and gave perhaps the shortest talk in the history of his school, but his words were profound. He said, "Never give in! Never give in! Never! Never! Never! Never!" Graham concluded by shouting to his audience, "And you today, pursue the vision, reach toward the goal, fulfill the dream, and as you move to do it, never, never, never give in."

16.

People of Other Faiths

THE SHORT, BROWN-HAIRED, middle-aged woman sat quietly in her seat as the plane flew through a tornado over Lake Michigan. In an hour Rivka Alexandrovich, a schoolteacher and recent immigrant from the Soviet Union, would meet the world-famous evangelist Billy Graham. This was not, however, to be a social call. Mrs. Alexandrovich's daughter, Ruth, was in jail in Russia as a result of her activities in trying to gain freedom for her fellow Jews. Two of Rivka's friends were taking her to meet Billy in the hope that he would be interested in her cause. When the plane landed at Chicago's O'Hare field Mrs. Alexandrovich and her friends taxied to the enormous Conrad Hilton Hotel on the lake front and rode an elevator to Graham's top floor room. Billy greeted the upset mother warmly,

and the two engaged in an intense half-hour conversation. Graham, who had long been interested in
the question of religious freedom in many parts of
the world, reacted positively to Mrs. Alexandrovich
and promised to do all he could to help gain her
daughter's release. Although he does not often make
public statements on international issues, Billy was
so moved by Rivka's story that he released a com-
ment from his Minneapolis headquarters that very
evening in which he called upon Christians to join
in prayer for Mrs. Alexandrovich's daughter and her
colleagues. Graham's statement also said, "I am
deeply concerned and disturbed about the plight of
Soviet Jews, some of whom have been imprisoned and
held incommunicado. Apparently their only crime is
that they are Jewish."

Graham's reaction to the plight of the Soviet
Jews, his keen interest in Israel, and his efforts to pro-
mote better understanding between the Christian and
Jewish communities mark him as a sincere and
highly significant worker in the area of interreligious
relations. He will not compromise his basic religious
views to win friends from other faiths, but he does
recognize the varied nature of American society, and
he desires harmony among the major American religious groups. In this area, as on many other sub-
jects, Graham has been a forward-looking evangelical
leader. The sad truth is that for much of the American experience evangelicals have expressed hostility
toward Jews, Roman Catholics, and others who did
not share their doctrines and values. This does not

mean that Graham is ecumenical in the current manner in which this word is used. He is not a part of the movement for union between the Roman Catholics and various Protestant denominations. He recognizes too many points of difference separating the various church bodies. He has particular difficulty in relating to the more liberal churches who, he feels, often dilute the gospel and stress social change at the expense of personal salvation. He has, however, supported dialogue between evangelicals and Jews, and between evangelicals and Roman Catholics. In 1969 he met with a group of Jewish leaders at the headquarters of the American Jewish Committee in New York. This session was marked by a frank and open discussion. A number of the Jewish participants were struck by Graham's openness to dialogue, notwithstanding the grave theological differences which exist between the evangelical Christian and Jewish communities. Rabbi Marc H. Tanenbaum, the Committee's National Director of Interreligious Affairs, praised Graham for contributions to a breakthrough in overcoming some of the misconceptions which existed in the Jewish community concerning evangelism. A year later Rabbi Tanenbaum attended one of the sessions at Billy Graham's Shea Stadium Crusade and expressed appreciation for the way the evangelist used the Old Testament as "a document with validity in its own right." He also noted that the concept of conversion so crucial to Graham's ministry was also emphasized in the thinking of many rabbis.

Graham's first major exposure to the Roman Catholic community occurred in 1963 when he was invited to address the student body at North Carolina's Belmont Abbey College. In his speech to a capacity crowd of 1,500 the evangelist hailed the late Pope John XXIII for bringing about new dialogue and understanding which could start a great Christian revolution. "This," he declared, "is the beginning of something so fantastic it could change all of Christendom and will affect you and future generations." Billy remarked to the students that his first talk at a Catholic institution was a very important experience for him and a very significant part of his ministerial career. Father John Oetgen, the president of the college, told the audience that the school had been praised for being the first Catholic institution to invite the famous evangelist to speak. "After hearing Dr. Graham talk we should be blamed for having waited so long," he said.

The next year Graham spoke to an enthusiastic audience of 5,000 students at Boston College, a Roman Catholic institution run by the Jesuit order. Graham was in the Massachusetts capital for a crusade. The day before, he had met with Richard Cardinal Cushing, the city's Roman Catholic archbishop. Billy had stopped by the Cardinal's residence to thank him for an editorial in the leading Catholic newspaper which welcomed him and the crusade to Boston. Cardinal Cushing had also urged Catholic college students in the region to attend the crusade, "because Billy Graham's message is one of Christ's crucifixion and no Catholic can do anything but become a better Catholic from hearing him." After meeting with Graham, the aging, but still forceful leader told a group of newsmen, "I am one hundred per cent for Billy Graham. He is extraordinarily gifted, and I only wish we had a half dozen men of his ability to go forth and preach the gospel." Twice during 1968, at both the Pittsburgh and San Antonio Crusades, Graham's activities were supported by local Roman Catholics. At San Antonio in June, Graham remarked that Roman Catholics had extended tremendous cooperation to his crusades and, he added, "a great part of our support today comes from Catholics. We never have a crusade now without priests and nuns being much in evidence in the audience." Just before the opening of the Pittsburgh Crusade, Bishop John Wright called upon the Catholic clergy and laity to pray for the Billy Graham Crusade. In a pastoral letter sent out to the churches in his diocese Bishop Wright wrote, "Even those who do not share other elements of the crusade's theology rejoice that a powerful voice will be lifted in Pittsburgh to proclaim the divinity of our Savior, Jesus Christ."

Later in the year, Graham was praised in the influential Catholic magazine, *The Lamp*. This periodical's editor, Father Charles Angell, cited Graham for his "updated appeal to the whole man and for unqualified dedication, total sincerity, charismatic appeal, and relevant preaching."

One of the most significant manifestations of Graham's work in building better relationships between evangelicals and Roman Catholics occurred during the massive evangelical campaign known as "Key 73." This effort, aimed at "confronting every person on the North American continent with the claims of Christ," saw Roman Catholics and evangelical Protestants joining together in several major cities in an attempt to witness their faith. For many of the persons involved, this was a first, and it set the stage for even more concentrated cooperation in the future.

17.

Concern for Young People

ANGRY SHOUTS, OBSCENE WORDS, and taunts filled the air as a tall man wearing thick-rimmed glasses and a deer-stalker's hat got out of a taxi cab near the entrance to the Columbia University campus. Columbia was undergoing a period of unrest, and Billy Graham had come to get a first hand look at the Columbia riots. Graham edged his way into the crowd of students surrounding the library. He soon came upon a group of young men who were trying to break into the building and within moments a squad of New York City policemen dressed in full battle gear broke up the crowd.

Graham chatted with several of the young people on the campus, and as he left to return to his downtown hotel, he expressed the fear that demonstrations like this would undermine the educational process.

Later, speaking on the CBS radio program "World of Religion," the evangelist was highly critical of student groups whose actions caused colleges to close. He expressed the thought that these actions were partly responsible for a trend toward the right within American society, and he warned that continued demonstrations and closings could lead to demands for suppression of certain civil liberties.

Billy has always been interested in education. A good portion of his yearly tithe goes to Christian colleges, and throughout the years he has remained particularly close to his alma mater, Wheaton College. During the height of campus unrest Graham held two long meetings with leaders of the Students for a Democratic Society, one of the more militant organizations operating on college and university campuses. In these meetings Graham tried to understand what was on the students' minds, but he also firmly stated his belief that rioting and demonstrations would not solve their problems. One evening when Billy was in New York, a radical student came to his hotel room for a conference. During the course of the conversation Graham asked the student what his goals were. At first the young man didn't reply. Then he walked over to the window and pointed at the Manhattan skyline. "What we want to do," he shouted, "is to tear this all down." Billy replied, "O.K. But what are you going to build in its place?" To this the student had no ready answer.

Graham, however, recognized the dedication of the campus radicals to their cause, and, speaking to a Madison Square Garden audience in 1969, he noted that this dedication was similar in type to that of the early Christians. Just a few days before, Billy had received a copy of a letter written by a student radical to his girlfriend. In the letter he told the young woman he was prepared to go before a firing squad to achieve his goals. Graham, commenting on the letter, said, "This sounds like the writing of the early church. Somewhere along the line we've lost the meaning of discipleship."

Graham's prescription for the unrest caused by the student movement was in keeping with his basic philosophy of life. In December of 1970 he spoke to the student body at Anderson–Montreat College just a few miles from his home. In this address he pointed out that in the student movement's search for new freedom there was the danger of the society losing what little freedom it had left. The evangelist concluded that a religious revival would be the only thing which could turn the tide and bring America to her senses.

By the end of the '60s Graham, along with many other Americans, was aware of the growing religious wave developing among many young people. Large numbers of high school and college students were aligning themselves with evangelical Christianity, although not necessarily with churches or established organizations. The Jesus People rejected the teaching and program of the student movement and substituted Christ as the answer to basic problems. The Jesus movement appeared to have its start on the

West Coast and then rapidly spread throughout the country. Some observers applauded the growth of this movement, while others were concerned with its anti-establishment tendencies and its excessive zeal. Graham attempted to steer an independent course in his reaction to the Jesus movement. He felt the young people who were now high on Jesus instead of on drugs, cults, and political activism were similar to other Christians throughout the ages who had rejected conventional activities and had developed their own strategies and life styles.

One day while Graham was on the West Coast for a crusade at the Anaheim, California, stadium, a reporter asked some probing questions about the Jesus People. Graham, who had met a number of these folk and whose mail was beginning to reflect their growing numbers and influence, told the newsman, "The rise of such movements as the Jesus Freaks and others is giving great encouragement to others. The mass media has been giving much attention to the rise of these groups, and although they are totally unconventional and, as they would say, 'doing their own thing,' this has been true at many times in the church's history. Small groups have arisen, shocking the established church, and yet retaining a very vivid hope in God." He went on to say that in his visits to many college and university campuses he had found students put off by the religious establishment and its various organizations. There were many devout young people in the colleges, but they had not as yet entered any established church. They seemed to have found Christ in their own way and were expressing their religious faith in a manner which both satisfied them emotionally and expressed their basic beliefs.

Graham's ministry has had a tremendous influence among young people. In recent years at least one, and in most cases two or more, meetings of the crusades are designated "Youth Night." In his rallies Billy makes a special point of preaching on themes related to the interests and problems of youth. Often famous athletes and other celebrities join Graham on the platform and testify to their faith in Christ. A school of evangelism is conducted at each crusade and most of the people in attendance are either seminary students or young pastors. These church workers come from the geographic region adjacent to the crusade city and spend a week in study, prayer, and fellowship. In a typical day the students listen to lectures by outstanding authorities, participate in workshops dealing with the practical elements of the ministry, and attend the nightly crusade meeting. This school of evangelism reflects Graham's tremendous interest in the clergy, and he makes a special point of addressing the student body during the week they spend at the crusade site. Graham, probably more than any other individual, is responsible for the large enrollments at the major evangelical theological seminaries. By the middle 1970s a number of Southern Baptist and inter-denominational schools were crammed with young men and women who had been converted as a result of Graham's evangelistic ministry. Billy's impact upon churches will last for generations after he has completed his active ministry.

18.

The Racial Struggle

DYNAMITE HILL is the name usually associated with the black section of Birmingham—Alabama's largest city, and the scene of considerable racial tension during the early 1960s. On Easter Sunday 1964, Legion Field, which lies at the foot of Dynamite Hill, was jammed with nearly 50,000 blacks and whites, the largest integrated audience ever assembled in Alabama. The occasion was a special religious service arranged by a bi-racial committee in an attempt to foster reconciliation between the races. Despite threats from the local White Citizens' Council, a segregationist group which called the meeting dangerous, Billy Graham came to Birmingham and from the Legion Field platform shouted, "What a moment and what an hour for Birmingham. It is good to stand together for Christ." The service was remarkable, especially in the light of the recent history of racial trouble in Birmingham. Only the year before, four black Sunday school girls had been killed when a bomb went off in their Baptist church. During the same year, police dogs and fire hoses put down demonstrations by blacks wanting equality. A local committee of Protestant, Roman Catholic, and Jewish clergymen, organized along inter-racial lines, decided late in 1963 to invite Graham to the city for a one-day meeting. This group had been particularly impressed by films of the Los Angeles Crusade showing blacks and whites worshiping together.

Graham, who was born in the South and who spent his formative years in that area of the country, had long been interested in race relations. In his early years he, like almost all young people who grew up in that region filled with the old-time religion, was taught that blacks were basically inferior to whites. It was not until he studied anthropology at Wheaton College that he learned of the equality of all races. His childhood experiences with blacks had been basically positive. Reese Brown, a black worker on his father's Charlotte dairy farm, had impressed Billy with his physical talents, his intelligence, and his efficient work habits. When Graham began his preaching career, most of his meetings were in the South. There the accepted pattern was segregated seating—with blacks and whites in different parts of an auditorium or stadium. At first the evangelist accepted this arrangement, but in 1953 he decided to conduct crusades only in sites where the audience would be integrated. During his crusade in Jackson, Mississippi, in June, 1953, the governor of that state telephoned Graham several times asking him to segregate the crowds who flocked to the crusade sessions. Graham refused. This was an act of some courage, considering that it took place in the city known as the "cradle of the Confederacy" and one of the main strongholds of segregation in the United States.

In 1957 Graham integrated his staff when Howard Jones, a Cleveland pastor and former missionary to Liberia, joined him for the New York Crusade. The next year Graham was barred from the Statehouse grounds in South Carolina by Governor George Timmerman, Jr., who said that Graham was "an advocate of desegregation." Governor Timmerman was probably referring to Graham's visits to Little Rock, Arkansas, in 1957 and Clinton, Tennessee, in 1958, both sites of racial strife related to the integration of public schools. Graham, in going to these cities, as well as to other areas torn by racial unrest, believed that he could play the role of reconciler. "I don't feel I have the whole answer," he told a reporter for the *New York Times,* "but at least for the time being as a Southerner I have a voice in the South, and I will try to provide the leadership I can."

One should also remember that in the 1940s and '50s when Graham was emerging as a widely recognized evangelical leader, evangelical Protestantism was overwhelmingly white and conservative in its views of race. Even as late as 1960 most evangelical colleges had few blacks among their student bodies. For example, the Moody Bible Institute of Chicago had only ten blacks in its student body of close to 1,000, and seven of these young people were visitors from African nations. When Graham was rising to a leadership position, few evangelical ministers had pulpit or personal fellowship with their black counterparts. Even though evangelicals stressed the capacity of the gospel to break down barriers between men, they went along with the prevailing attitudes toward race in both the South and the North.

In May of 1965, speaking at the University of North Carolina, Graham made what was thought to be his strongest statement up to that time on the racial issue. He told the 16,000 persons gathered in Kenon Stadium: "These people who say they can prove segregation from the Bible don't know their Bible. The real message of the Bible is 'Love thy neighbor as thyself.' "

The next month Graham conducted an eight-day crusade in Montgomery, Alabama—a city known throughout the nation as a symbol of resistance to racial change. Montgomery had attracted world-wide attention as a result of the recent civil rights march led by Dr. Martin Luther King, Jr. Dr. King had preached an eloquent sermon in front of the Alabama State Capitol Building moments after the completion of a march through the heart of the state. Graham's visit to Montgomery had been preceded by opposition from the White Citizens' Councils, who suggested that Graham's visit to Alabama was made with the intention of stirring up trouble. The Councils were responsible for starting a rumor which suggested that President Lyndon B. Johnson had "sent" the evangelist to Alabama. Graham responded by saying, "I am here at the invitation of religious and civic leaders. No one told me to come except the Lord."

There is little doubt that Graham's ministry suffered as a result of his strong stand on improving race relations. Speaking in Honolulu before the University of Hawaii Campus Conference on Religion, Graham said, "I lost supporters, received threats and angry letters because of my stand on race, but segregation is wrong. If Christ came back here he probably wouldn't be able to get into some churches because he wasn't white."

19.

An Influence for Change

AT THE CONCLUSION of the Montgomery Crusade Graham told an interviewer, "If this sort of Christian love continues to prevail, then I foresee the day when all America will point to Alabama with pride on the racial question. What a thrill it was to hear an interracial choir of 1,000 voices sing 'How Great Thou Art,' and enjoy it. What a thrill to see the thousands sitting side by side listening to the gospel. Night after night I watched thousands of them worship, people of both races, not with hatred but with unity and a spirit of love, and Christ drew them together. As we watched this thrilling sight one of the pastors on the platform whispered, 'This is the answer to our problem,' and I've always understood that the first sign a person has that he is truly in Christ is his awareness of equality."

Graham's visit to Alabama did have a widespread impact. The Reverend Clayton Bell, minister of the First Presbyterian Church of Dothan, said the meetings conducted by Graham were the first interracial sessions in the city's history. "Not only was there no conflict, but a general spirit of love and fellowship captivated the hearts of those present," Bell added.

Two months after the Montgomery Crusade the nation was stunned by a violent racial outburst in the Watts section of southcentral Los Angeles. Billy heard the news while resting at his Montreat home. He flew immediately to the strife-torn city where he was greeted by Governor Edmund Brown and taken for a helicopter tour of the riot area. He later told newsmen that he believed extremists played a major role in provoking the disturbance. Graham's analysis of the situation seemed to reflect the sentiments of most Americans when he said, "I believe the riots have hurt the civil rights cause. People across the nation are afraid, baffled, and bewildered by what happened in Los Angeles." Graham believed that the riots could not have occurred without proper planning and organization, and he appealed to the government to identify those groups teaching and advocating violence. Speaking on "The Hour of Decision" he said, "The majority of the American people want law, order, and security. There is no doubt the rioting in America this summer has reached the point of anarchy."

During the remainder of the 1960s, Graham advocated moderation in dealing with the nation's racial ills. He supported legislation aimed at helping blacks achieve legal, social, and economic opportunity, but he cautioned against the kind of activism which he felt, in the long run, could only hurt the cause. At the same time, he added a number of talented blacks to his staff and urged his fellow evangelicals to pay closer attention to the needs of the black community. Graham himself became more fully aware of the problems confronted by blacks through a meeting with a well-informed Los Angeles black minister, Dr. Edward V. Hill. Hill, who now serves on the board of directors of the Billy Graham Evangelistic Association, met Graham during the 1969 Anaheim, California, Crusade. "I was sitting behind Billy on the platform," he recalls, "and I had this urge to tap him on the shoulder and ask him for an appointment. Yet another voice kept telling me, 'why Billy Graham's too busy and too important to have any time for you.' The spirit finally moved me and I leaned forward and said, 'Dr. Graham, I've got to talk to you.' Billy turned around and said, 'I've got to talk to you too.'"

A few days later the two men met for what was supposed to be a half hour briefing session. Hill ended up spending over six hours with the evangelist talking about the problems of blacks. He told Graham about the unrest which existed among black evangelicals and their impatience with their white brothers who appeared to have little interest in their problems. Ever since that meeting, Hill has appeared with Graham at his major crusades and has been an important force in forging closer ties between Graham and black church leaders.

In the spring of 1975 Hill traveled to Jackson, Mississippi, to prepare the black community for Graham's mid-May crusade. His last visit to the Mississippi capital had been as a Freedom Rider in the early 1960s, and he and his associates had an extremely difficult time with the local authorities. During the 1975 Jackson Crusade, Hill worked out of the Graham headquarters in a downtown hotel, and he remembered, "It's a long way from this Hilton to where I stayed during the Freedom Rider days."

Future historians looking back upon mid-twentieth century America will likely assign an important role to Billy Graham as an agent of racial change. While Graham has been criticized by some of his contemporaries for not going far enough on the subject of race, he has been a major force for good in promoting racial goodwill. As historians examine his activities and statements from 1950 on, they will conclude that he was surely not silent, or even cautious, on the racial question. Further, when they consider his background, following, and the mood of the nation during the period, they will likely feel that he was well ahead of the rest of his fellow Americans on this crucial issue. Future scholars will also understand the limitations that Graham faced. He did not hold political office, nor did he have an official church-related post. His vast influence was based on his career as an evangelist and his personal integrity.

In evaluating Graham's contributions on the subject of race relations one must remember that his basic theological orientation kept him from taking the kind of activistic position that some more radical churchmen advocated. In evaluating Graham's actions it must be realized that he firmly believes that real social change can come only when the majority of society has experienced personal redemption. To Graham, racial prejudice is a symptom of man's sinful nature and can never be understood or treated apart from that. "Only when men stand together at the cross do real barriers fully come down." In his bestselling book, *World Aflame,* published during the midst of the nation's racial crisis, Graham wrote, "The race problem, and all other problems, can be solved, but only at the cross. The cross of Christ is not only the basis of our peace and hope; but it is also the means of our eternal salvation. The object of the cross is not only a full and free pardon; it is also a changed live lived in fellowship with God. This is the Christian message for the world today. This is the message of hope and peace and brotherhood."

20.

Inside the White House

HARRY TRUMAN was known as a man of strong opinions, and he very seldom hid his views from the public. Today he was particularly opinionated about a certain North Carolina preacher and evangelist who had just come to call upon him in the White House. Soon after the minister left his office Truman called in one of his aides and exploded, "I never want to see that son-of-a-gun again, and you'd better not invite him to this house or *you'll* never see me again."

The president had enjoyed meeting Billy Graham. The two men had spent an hour or so discussing national problems, and their conversation also included some personal matters. When the talk was over Truman said to Graham, "Now remember, this has been an off-the-record discussion and I'm counting on you to keep my comments private." Two hours later the teletype machine in the White House carried a long story based on an interview Graham gave to reporters when he left the executive mansion. It seems that Billy, Grady Wilson, and one or two other associates walked out into the sunshine of the rose garden and got down on their knees for a word of prayer. Several quick-witted reporters, looking through the windows of the White House press office, saw the Graham party and ran out to question them about their chat with the president. This was a new experience for Graham. It was the first time he had ever met with a president, and he began to re-count in detail everything he and Truman had discussed. Graham learned an important lesson from this experience, and although he was never to meet with Truman again while the Missourian served as chief executive, he would go on to become the close friend of a number of presidents, from Dwight D. Eisenhower to Gerald R. Ford.

Shortly before Truman's successor, General Dwight David Eisenhower, was inaugurated, Billy was called to the president-elect's New York hotel suite for a conference. The president-elect told Billy that he would like to include a Bible passage in his inaugural address. Billy suggested a number of possibilities, including the verse in 2 Chronicles which Eisenhower later used in his speech. During the Eisenhower years Billy was invited to the White House several times, but he and the former military hero did not become close friends until after Eisenhower left office. Graham was one of the last people to speak to the ex-president while he lay dying in the Walter Reed Army Hospital, and on the day of Eisenhower's funeral his widow, Mamie, invited Billy to her home for a private conversation. Graham and Mrs. Eisenhower have remained good friends in the intervening years.

Graham first met President Kennedy when the latter was a senator, and he played a minor role in the controversy over Kennedy's Roman Catholic affiliation, which marred the 1960 presidential campaign. Graham joined with a group of prominent Protestant clergy who raised questions concerning the potential influence of the Pope on Kennedy's decision-making. Actually, Graham was not closely involved with this group and did not attend a widely reported session critical of Kennedy chaired by the prominent New York City clergyman, Dr. Norman Vincent Peale. It might be remembered that Kennedy himself put an end to the issue by confronting a group of Houston, Texas, clergymen and answering their questions concerning his religious background. After Kennedy's election, Graham played several rounds of golf with him and visited the young national leader in the White House and at Kennedy's Palm Beach, Florida, home. After Kennedy's untimely death Billy told a North Carolina audience six things he had learned from the former president's life: the value of seeking knowledge and understanding; the value of tireless work; the need for racial understanding; the urgency of the world situation; the need for religious tolerance in a varied society; and the shortness of life.

21.

LBJ

THE TWO FRIENDS left the ranch house and walked out into the hot sun. The stockier of the two men guided the other to a plot of ground near a small but swiftly flowing river. "This is where I want to be buried, and I want you to preach at my funeral," the man said. These words were said with great emotion, and Billy Graham felt deeply moved as he listened to the President of the United States. He watched intently as Lyndon Johnson kneeled and ran his hands over the hard Texas earth. Some years later the evangelist would return to the spot to officiate at Johnson's funeral, and he would recall the look in his friend's eyes as he spoke of the land, the nearby hills and the immense Texas blue sky.

Graham and Kennedy's successor, Lyndon Baines Johnson, had a lot in common: they were both

Southerners and felt a tremendous sense of allegiance
to their home region. The two men were extremely
close. In a sense, Graham, although only ten years
younger than Johnson, was regarded by the president
as almost a son, or certainly a close member of the
family. Billy spent many nights in the White House
during the Johnson administration and was an important counselor on many vital issues. This was
not a role that Graham sought for himself, but rather
it was something which Johnson began. A typical
Graham visit to the White House during the Johnson
years included conversation, a dip in the White House
pool, dinner, prayer and Bible study. One of Johnson's top aides, Bill D. Moyers, a graduate of the
Southwestern Baptist Theological Seminary and an
ordained Southern Baptist minister, often joined the
two men during their lengthy conversations.

The day before Johnson ran for re-election against
Arizona Senator Barry Goldwater, Graham received
sixty thousand telegrams at his Montreat home urging him to back Goldwater. This incredible avalanche
of communication made the opening of five extra
wires at the Ashville Western Union office necessary
and caused the normal staff and a number of temporary helpers to work around the clock. Despite
the pressure produced by the messages, which flowed
in from every part of the United States, Graham
remained neutral and did not endorse either candidate.

Actually, however, some observers believed that
Graham's failure to back the Republican Goldwater

110

amounted to an endorsement of President Johnson. These experts pointed out that under normal circumstances Graham's followers would have been expected to back the more conservative Goldwater, but that Graham's continuing association with Johnson obviously caused a number of his supporters to feel that the evangelist favored LBJ.

Once, for example, Bill Moyers received a telephone call from a Southern Baptist leader who protested Mr. Johnson's civil rights position and said that he could never support such a man. The caller also demanded to speak to the president. Moyers responded that Mr. Johnson would have to return the call because at that very moment he was swimming with Billy Graham in the White House pool. The Baptist leader was silent for a moment, and then quietly said perhaps it wasn't necessary for the president to call him back after all.

One of Mr. Johnson's favorite anecdotes about the evangelist concerned the time that the two men had a round of mutual backslapping. The president told Billy that he thought he was the nation's greatest religious leader, while Graham said to the president that he was certainly the greatest political leader of the twentieth century. A few days later one of Graham's daughters announced that she was voting for Barry Goldwater. The president, upon hearing this news, telephoned Billy and said, "You may be a great religious leader, but you can't influence your own family in politics." Then some weeks later, Luci Johnson, the president's younger daughter, revealed that she was going to join the Roman Catholic Church. Billy telephoned Mr. Johnson and said, "You may be a great political leader, but you don't seem to have much influence over your family's religious life."

Interestingly enough, Billy Graham would probably make an outstanding political leader. He has all of the characteristics one would usually feel are necessary in a political chieftain. He is an excellent speaker, and his personality and intelligence would hold him in good stead if he chose to seek elected office. Back in the 1950s a group of important North Carolinians urged him to run for the United States Senate, but Billy refused. He told the group that he was highly flattered by the invitation, but he believed his basic calling was to preach the gospel.

Over the years there have also been reports indicating that each of the major parties would welcome Graham's offering himself as a presidential candidate. Graham, who is a registered Democrat, has never taken any of these offers seriously, although given his tremendous popularity one suspects he could wage a very strong race for the nation's highest office.

Graham was Mr. Johnson's guest during LBJ's last weekend in the White House, and he remained close to the Texan throughout the rest of Johnson's life. The evangelist preached the sermon at the ex-president's funeral, and he later remarked, "I have known and loved him as a personal friend and had the rare privilege of spending many hours with him at the White House, in Texas, and at Camp David. He was a deeply religious man who could not forget his Christian heritage. He probably attended church more than any other president in our history."

22.

The Senator from California

IT WAS A WARM SPRING DAY in 1950 and two men who had met just a few hours before were golfing at Washington's Burning Tree Country Club. One man was a United States Senator, the other, a well-known evangelist. In the years to follow the paths of Richard M. Nixon of California and Billy Graham of North Carolina would cross many times.

Graham offered a lengthy prayer at the inauguration of Johnson's successor, Richard M. Nixon. Graham and Nixon have known each other since 1950. They met while Graham was having lunch in the senate dining room, and the two men saw each other from time to time when Mr. Nixon served in the senate and when he was vice-president under Dwight Eisenhower. Nixon was a featured speaker at the last Yankee Stadium rally during the 1957

New York City Crusade. Actually, Graham knew Nixon's parents before he ever met the California political leader. Nixon's mother and father were evangelical Quakers and supporters of Paul Rader, a well-known evangelist of the 1930s. Mrs. Nixon was a deeply religious woman and her son recalled that he made a decision for Christ when he was twelve at a Paul Rader revival. After 1960 when Nixon practiced law in California and later in New York, he and Graham met several times a year and talked about world events. The two men enjoyed playing golf together, and once Nixon sent the evangelist a box of golf balls with the name "Nixon" engraved on them. Billy apparently had bad luck with this gift because Nixon later told him that people kept finding the monogrammed balls in the rough and in out-of-bounds areas.

In November of 1962 Nixon published an article in *Decision* magazine in which he said "the strength of a nation's faith in God can be measured only in terms of the faith of each of its individual citizens." Late in 1967 Nixon telephoned Graham asking the evangelist to join him in Florida where the former vice-president was deciding whether or not to run for the presidency in 1968. Nixon and Graham spent hours walking on the beach, praying, and studying the Bible. Nixon later gave credit to Graham for being a determining factor in his decision to run for the nation's highest office.

This decision was to have an important influence on the course of Graham's public career. While

Graham continued to state his long-held policy of refusing to endorse any candidate for major political office, he did seem to agree philosophically with Nixon. Despite the claim that his involvement in party politics would "greatly diminish my ministry," he did mail a letter to his followers which seemed to support Nixon. The letter, which was sent from Minneapolis in mid-August, started out by suggesting that Graham would take the advice of his friends, Richard Nixon and Lyndon Johnson, to stay out of politics. The letter went on to say that "my commitments and sympathies are strong this year, and it will be difficult to keep quiet when I feel so deeply. However, I am praying that the man of God's choice will be elected." Many of the people who received this letter, as well as neutral observers, sensed that between the lines Graham was saying that he believed Nixon was the chosen candidate.

The next month Nixon was a platform guest during the Pittsburgh Crusade, and he and his wife were introduced to an enthusiastic audience. About the best his rival, Hubert H. Humphrey, could do was to send a telegram of greeting to Graham, supporting his work in the Steel City.

In October, as the campaign heated up, some Democrats attacked Nixon's character and personal integrity. Graham issued a statement defending Nixon saying, "I can testify that he is a man of high moral principles, and while I do not intend to endorse any political candidate publicly, I maintain the right to help put the record straight when a friend is smeared." As the campaign wound to a close, the pressures on Graham to speak out in favor of Nixon were very strong, and on October 17 he told an interviewer, "I am trying to stay totally out of politics, and I intend to go into complete hiding for the last week of the campaign."

On election day Nixon squeaked through to victory in one of the closest presidential elections in American history. Shortly after his election Nixon held Sunday morning religious services in the White House, and Graham was invited to be the first speaker. Several important clergymen criticized these White House services, believing that they were a violation of the traditional American concept of separation of church and state. Graham, however, felt that the majority of Americans were happy about services in the president's house.

There is little doubt that Graham's friendship with Nixon deepened during the Californian's first term in office. Graham was reported as saying, "It is wonderful for a clergyman to have a friendship with a president." The two men met and talked with each other often. During one three-week period in the spring of 1969, Graham flew with Nixon in Air Force 1 to a dedication ceremony, took part in a meeting of the Richard Nixon Foundation, stayed at the western White House in San Clemente, California, was one of two clergymen invited by Nixon to attend a dinner honoring the astronauts, and golfed with the president.

During the next year, something happened which

117

had far-reaching effects on Graham's relationship to the presidency. In May of 1970 Graham conducted a major crusade on the campus of the University of Tennessee at Knoxville. Two days after the crusade started Nixon phoned Graham from the White House and invited himself to one of the crusade sessions. Graham could hardly refuse to have the president come, even though the excuse for the visit was rather flimsy. Nixon told the evangelist he was stopping off on his way to his home in Key Biscayne, Florida. Graham, who has traveled throughout the United States, realized that the shortest route between Washington and southern Florida did not run through east Tennessee, but there was little he could do to prevent Nixon from showing up. Nixon's purpose in coming to Knoxville was to support the candidacy of William Brock, who was at that time engaged in a fierce struggle to unseat Democratic Senator Albert Gore. Brock sat next to Nixon on the platform while Gore later claimed that he did not receive an invitation to the crusade. On the night of May 28, Nixon appeared at the Knoxville Crusade and gave a long address identifying himself with Graham's cause. While the president spoke, a crowd of chanting demonstrators tried to disrupt the meeting. A number of arrests were made, and the court cases resulting from this incident took several years to be settled. When news of the episode spread across the country, even some of Graham's most loyal supporters felt that Graham had been used by Nixon strictly for political ends.

Graham remained close to Nixon over the course

of the next year and in June of 1971, while in Chicago for a crusade, said of Nixon, "I have great admiration for him. I think he's the best trained man for the presidency in this century. The fact that he kept the country together is really an amazing thing. I try to stay out of partisan politics, in fact just recently I was the main speaker at the opening of the Lyndon Johnson Library. Of course," he laughed, "I flew down in Air Force 1 with President Nixon."

The very fact, however, that Graham had a positive relationship with Nixon allowed him to have some influence on issues of particular concern to the evangelist. Graham was responsible for setting up a White House meeting at which a number of black clergymen engaged in a frank discussion with Nixon concerning domestic problems. This session resulted in the Nixon administration freeing significant sums of money for federally-related programs and projects in the various black communities across the country. When the Watergate affair broke, Graham at first refused to be drawn into the controversy, but as evidence of Nixon's guilt mounted, Graham spoke out in an article on the opinion page of the *New York Times*. In this article Graham appeared to say that the welfare and unity of the country was of greater concern than the career of any one political leader. Graham's comments angered Nixon and put a serious strain on their longstanding friendship. When the White House tapes were published, Graham was shocked at the language employed by Nixon in conversations in the Oval Office. But he did support President Ford's pardon of Nixon. In discussing Ford's action, Graham said, "Nixon has already paid a terrible price for the mistakes of his administration. Except for Watergate, Nixon served his country with great distinction, and I believe history will so judge."

Graham, who is a very forgiving man, is always prepared to give individuals the benefit of the doubt. He had mixed feelings about Nixon. On the one hand, he realized Nixon's responsibility for the Watergate fiasco, but at the same time, Nixon was an old friend, and Billy simply could not desert him in a time of great trouble. There was no question that their relationship had cooled and would probably never be the same, but in the months following Nixon's return to California, Graham visited him and attempted to provide spiritual comfort. It is quite likely that Graham's experience with President Nixon will make him more cautious in dealing with future chief executives.

Part Three

Billy Graham–The Man and
Evangelical Leader

23.

At Home in Montreat

AN ATTRACTIVE MIDDLE-AGED COUPLE holding hands and thoroughly relaxed with each other sat reading. The woman, once described by her college house-mother as having "the most beautiful Christian character of any young person I have ever known," and the man, the world's most famous evangelist, were enjoying a rare moment of quiet. For most of their married life Ruth and Billy Graham have experienced weeks and months of separation from each other; he, busy preaching in far-off places; she, occupied with raising their family of five active children. Now, with their children grown and the evangelist's schedule not as hectic as it used to be, there is more opportunity for this lovely couple to be together.

Mrs. Graham has had some exciting experiences in her own right. She has floated over Acapulco dangling from a parachute towed by a speedboat. She has tried hang-gliding and has made attempts to learn to ride a motorcycle. All of this has been in the last few years when, in her own words, she has been "getting on, no longer young."

"I had always thought it would be fun to ride a motorcycle," she said in an interview with Jeannette Branin of Copley News Service. "I do love to go fast, to go full speed with the wind in my face.

"I tried three times and had three disasters."

The first attempt ended when she drove through a rail fence; the second, when she turned the accelerator control instead of the brake control and ran off the road into a lake. The third and last attempt ended when she slid down the side of a mountain.

"What I really needed was to be on the Salt Flats in Utah," she said. "I could have gone top speed there and still had five miles to make a turn."

For many years Ruth and Billy have lived in Montreat, a tiny town nestled in the Blue Ridge Mountains of western North Carolina. Billy's boyhood home of Charlotte is a two-hour drive away—less when Billy is frantically trying to catch a plane from the Charlotte airport. Montreat was the home of Ruth's parents, Dr. and Mrs. L. Nelson Bell. The Bells came there after long years of missionary service in China. When the Grahams first married, they lived in a small house across from the Bells.

Then as their family grew Billy and Ruth built a home on the top of the mountain. This rustic house is constructed of old timber and has great charm; it radiates the warmth of its occupants.

The house also provides privacy for Billy, who travels a good part of the year and needs a place to rest. The remote location affords security from the many people who would like to get close to Billy and seek his interest on some project or personal matter. Graham is the most generous of men, and his staff is constantly coping with the out-workings of his generosity. He is also a world-famous celebrity and has to work at insuring some privacy for himself and his family. Billy loves to roam around the mountaintop, and he and Ruth often go for long walks in the countryside, especially in spring and autumn.

Montreat also provides a place for sermon and crusade preparation and the study necessary for Graham to keep abreast of changing intellectual and social patterns. Billy also conducts business from Montreat. He has an office in a building at the foot of the mountain but normally works out of his study in the house or greets guests in front of the fireplace in his large, comfortable living room. Ruth, a highly sophisticated and charming woman, often joins in the conversation and makes guests feel completely at ease.

On an average day at home Billy takes fifty or so telephone calls, talks with his key aides at his business office in Minneapolis and the team headquarters in Atlanta, and confers with government leaders from the United States and foreign nations. He reads, dictates mail, and studies reports concerning the operation of his world-wide organization. While he has a professional, competent, and loyal staff, Billy makes the major decisions involving the Billy Graham Evangelistic Association. He also has the last word on his busy schedule. He determines which invitations to hold city-wide crusades will be accepted and what individual speaking dates will be executed. This is no small problem considering the fact that he receives thousands of such invitations each year.

Graham is head of a major organization. He functions as a chief executive and is responsible to a board of directors which meets each month to evaluate the activities of the organization. Graham feels responsible to those who contribute financially to his work. Every year, fifteen to twenty million dollars flow into the Minneapolis office. Each donation is carefully recorded, and a receipt is sent to the giver. Graham studies the organization's expenditures carefully. He wants to be sure that every dollar spent is for a worthwhile purpose. George Wilson, who has introduced the latest technology in an attempt to deal efficiently with the ever-expanding facets of Graham's ministry, supports Billy in his business dealings. All of Graham's work is conducted on the highest ethical and moral level. This is one of the main reasons for his successful career, yet to truly understand Graham's incredible rise to fame, one must look at the underlying causes.

24.

Reasons for Graham's Success

WHILE BILLY GRAHAM is an ordained Baptist minister and holds honorary doctor's degrees from several educational institutions, he prefers to be called "Mr. Graham." Actually, he likes to be referred to as an evangelist. In a statement he issued in 1973 Graham said, "I am convinced that God has called me to be a New Testament evangelist, not an Old Testament prophet. While some may interpret an evangelist to be primarily a social reformer or a political activist, I don't! An evangelist is a proclaimer of the message of God's love and grace in Jesus Christ and the necessity of repentance and faith."

In this statement Graham places himself squarely in the mainstream of historic American evangelism. The first major American evangelist was Jonathan

Edwards, a highly educated and passionately motivated preacher, who brought about a series of important revivals in pre-revolutionary New England. Edwards was pastor of a Northampton, Massachusetts, church and from this base toured New England bringing many people to Christ. The next great U.S. evangelist was Charles Graddison Finney, also a man of immense learning and an effective preacher. Finney was president of Oberlin College in Ohio and was part of the revival movement which swept the Midwest and South in the 1850s. Finney was followed by D. L. Moody, a self-educated shoe salesman with a tremendous concern for soul winning. Moody toured America and England, often accompanied by the outstanding musician and hymn writer, Ira Sankey. Moody's ministry reached its peak in the last quarter of the nineteenth century. He was succeeded by Billy Sunday, a former baseball player whose fiery sermons and emotionally charged services marked evangelism in the period after World War I. All of these important evangelists spoke to large audiences and were responsible for the conversion of thousands of people, but none had the impact of Billy Graham. There are many ways of explaining why Graham has been the most successful American evangelist, but the period in which he became famous, his methods, and the development of the mass media are the most important factors.

Graham came to prominence immediately following World War II. These years were marked by crisis abroad and tension at home. Although many people thought the war's end would result in permanent peace and prosperity, they were disappointed. Instead, life seemed even more complex and difficult than before the war. People searched for answers in a world where there seemed to be only questions. Books on peace of mind and peace of soul were popular, but few people could seem to find inner peace. Newspapers were filled with stories of bloodshed in different parts of the globe, and the Soviet Union, our staunch ally in the war against Nazism, now became a feared enemy. By 1950 the Soviets had the capacity to manufacture the hydrogen bomb and were threatening to launch a war in Asia. The American people were confused, and political demagogues, such as the late Senator Joseph R. McCarthy of Wisconsin, chased around the country claiming to find communists in the government, the universities, and just about everywhere. The more liberal churches, those who stressed social action and put forth the belief that man could improve the world and himself by trying to do good, were losing favor. People realized that the world was not getting better; if anything it was becoming worse. Liberal churches had been saying throughout the first part of the twentieth century that man was going to bring about a just society, and that the kingdom of God would come to earth if men worked together for good. Graham challenged this theory and claimed that society could be changed for the better only when individual men and women confessed their sins and by faith accepted Jesus as Savior and Lord.

Once a person experienced the new birth, he or she would take on the fruits of the spirit: love, joy, long-suffering, patience, mercy. These redeemed individuals would bring about positive social change. At the heart of Graham's message to the American people, heard on hundreds of radio stations and preached to thousands of persons in stadiums and indoor arenas in most of the nation's largest cities, was the good news, the message that "Christ died for our sins, was buried and rose again the third day." This message, aimed at a confused and weary populace, had great impact. Graham was telling people that while they could not personally solve the world's ills, they could find peace with God (the title of his best-selling book), and thus be better equipped to confront life's complexities, difficulties, and problems.

Graham was able to very effectively get this message across as a result of the methods he devised. He formed an organization which operated with great skill and on the highest level of integrity. He also brought together the various elements of evangelical Christianity as no man before had done. Some of the extreme believers, men like Billy's old college president, Bob Jones, and the well-known evangelist, John R. Rice, did not support Graham's work; however, most evangelical leaders rallied behind Graham. Graham made evangelicalism respectable. This was no little achievement since as late as 1925 the famous Scopes trial, involving the question of the teaching of the theory of evolution in the public schools, had caused evangelicals to be the object of scorn and derision within American society. Graham's activities began to change this attitude. As he began to experience success, he gave heart to other evangelicals and enabled them to realize that a new climate was developing in the nation—one which took the preaching of the gospel seriously. In 1950 a new organization, the National Association of Evangelicals, was created to unify the evangelical movement and to challenge the older liberalism. Graham was at the center of this organization, and later exercised further leadership by being the driving force behind national and international conferences of evangelicals. Three such meetings were held between 1960 and 1974 in Minneapolis, Minnesota; Berlin, West Germany; and Lausanne, Switzerland. Graham, along with his father-in-law, the late L. Nelson Bell, was responsible for the founding of the highly popular evangelical magazine, *Christianity Today*.

One of the most important factors in Graham's success was his strategy of city-wide meetings and his inclusion of clergy of many denominations in the crusade efforts. His extremist critics attacked Graham for joining forces with liberal mainline clergy, but Graham argued that by getting the acceptance of the majority of the churches in a community, he was able to more effectively reach more people with the gospel message. Many of these more liberal clergy and their parishioners have become evangelicals as a result of Graham's ministry.

Another major factor in Graham's rise to prominence in the early 1950s was his skillful employment of the mass media. The "Hour of Decision" radio program made him a national, and then world-renowned, personality. Later he televised crusade meetings and aired them in strategic areas throughout the world. In using radio and television Graham was honest, and non-manipulative. The "Hour of Decision" had the same plan: an introduction by Cliff Barrows, Scripture reading by Grady Wilson, two hymns from George Beverly Shea, prayer, announcements, and then a sermon by Graham. The television programs have much the same format, with the added feature of being able to see Graham as he preaches. In recent years famous Christian entertainers and political figures have joined in the TV shows, but the focus of the programs is always on a clear presentation of the gospel message. Graham is also the subject of countless newspaper and magazine interviews. He is very skilled at fielding questions from even the most hostile journalists. In all of his public statements Graham never misses the opportunity of telling his basic spiritual beliefs.

25.

What Does
Billy Graham Believe?

BILLY GRAHAM'S basic beliefs are in line with the theological principles which have formed the basis of twentieth century evangelicalism. These beliefs include the inspiration and authority of the Bible, the virgin birth, the necessity of accepting Christ as personal Lord and Savior, the bodily resurrection of Jesus, and Christ's second coming.

Graham is especially concerned with the doctrine of salvation through Christ, and his ministry puts particular stress on the need of men to recognize their sinfulness and to accept Jesus as Lord and Savior. It is his gift to bring men to the point where in submission to God they recognize their utter dependence on Christ's work at the cross and allow Jesus to come into their lives, to bring salvation. To Graham, all people are sinners, not only through inheritance—that is, by Adam's fall—but also by choice. Sin is failure to live up to God's standards and keeps men from fellowship with God. Sin has a negative impact upon an individual's life, personality, and human relationships. It affects the mind, will, and conscience. So much so, Graham has written, "that the totality of life is infected, darkening his intellect, enfeebling his will, corrupting his emotions." Man as a sinner is alienated from God and in need of restoration. Sin causes physical, spiritual, and eternal death. The remedy for the effects of sin, as preached by Graham throughout his long career, is the redemption achieved by Christ. If persons will believe they will be saved and will take on a new outlook and life style. This "new birth," as it's called, is not simply a reformation, but a transformation. The redeemed man receives a new nature and a new heart and becomes a new creation. The new birth, therefore, is a radical and revolutionary phenomenon. It changes a person—he or she takes on the fruits of the spirit: joy, peace, patience, long-suffering, love, mercy, justice. The redeemed persons wait with keen anticipation for the second coming. This event will bring about the end of life as it is now known and will mark the beginning of a new and eternal age of peace and happiness. According to Graham, the second coming will be a totally revolutionary experience. It will "change every aspect of life on this planet. Christ will reign in righteousness. Disease will be arrested. Death will be modified. War will be abolished. Nature will be changed. Man will live as it was originally intended he should live." Graham believes that there are many current signs which point to the return of Christ. These are war, violence, lawlessness, immorality, persecution of those who believe in Christ, and an increase in mass evangelism to world-wide proportions.

Billy Graham's preaching thus stresses the evangelical teaching concerning the second coming of Christ. In every crusade he devotes at least one sermon to this theme. In his many interviews, letters, and in private conversation both with world leaders and with everyday people, Graham continually discusses the second coming. Along with most of his evangelical colleagues, Graham believes that the second coming could occur at any time. He believes that there are many signs that Christ's coming is near, and he constantly points to world events to back up this assertion. When Graham thinks about the second coming he is weighted down by a sense of urgency. He feels the need to reach every person he possibly can with the message of salvation before Jesus returns to the earth. At times he has been criticized for instilling a sense of fear in his listeners. His warnings concerning the second coming and God's ultimate judgment on the world are often accompanied by the warning that time is short, and his audience may never again have the opportunity to be saved. He is simply putting stress on Paul's teaching that "now is the time of salvation." Graham's preoccupation with the second coming of Christ has led some of his critics to say that the evangelist is not concerned enough with contemporary problems and the life activities of the world's people. While it is true that many evangelical Christians could be fairly criticized for having an almost completely other-worldly view of society, Graham has been able to successfully balance his belief in the second coming with genuine concern for current issues.

Some time ago Billy wrote:

The second coming must be viewed first of all as an historical event yet to take place. It is also the nature of a hope that has been given to Christians, and in anticipation of this hope God had given great encouragement to his church, particularly in times of extreme suffering and need. The second coming, therefore, has a timeless quality about it and it is with this in mind that I can feel so free in proclaiming the second coming of Christ as being a glorious hope given to the church without the necessity of establishing a date. Having said this, it is of the very nature of Christian concern that we become aware of social needs and wherever possible we do all that can be done to alleviate the suffering of humanity. This is a matter of Christian principle. And also the Christian is a citizen of two worlds. He is a citizen of this world in which he is now living, and living here he has certain responsibility. . . . Therefore in becoming politically involved and having a tremendous interest in our nation's well-being I cannot help but feel that this is rendering to Caesar the things that are Caesar's. I have this as a Christian responsibility as does every Christian . . . to become very much involved in the alleviation of the suffering of humanity through personal involvement and also retaining that blessed hope of the glorious appearing of our great God and Savior Jesus Christ.

Once Billy's tremendous concern for the second coming resulted in a rather amusing incident. Billy had arrived at the Charlotte airport after an out-of-town engagement and was picked up by T. W. Wilson, his old friend and close associate. Billy was rather tired and climbed into the back seat of the car and fell asleep. About an hour later, T. W. stopped for gas and Billy awoke and, without telling his friend, left the car to stretch his legs. T. W., thinking that Billy was still in the car, resumed driving and an hour or so later arrived at Billy's home in Montreat. He got out of the car and was amazed to find that Billy was not there. It then flashed through his mind that the second coming had taken place, and he had been left behind. His fears, however, were slightly eased when he knocked on Billy's front door and found that Ruth Graham had also remained behind.

In the meantime, after T. W. drove off, Billy went in to the little coffee shop next to the service station and asked the owner if he could find him a ride home. The proprietor asked his name, and

Billy, wearing dark glasses, an old golf cap, and clothes rumpled from sleeping in the rear of the auto, replied, "Why, I'm Billy Graham." To which the cafe owner said, "Yes, and I'm George Washington." It wasn't until Billy called the owner of a local motel, who convinced the restaurant owner that the sloppy-looking man was indeed the world-famous evangelist, that Billy got a ride home. When he reached Montreat, T. W. Wilson was even happier than Ruth to see him.

26.

At a Crusade

BILLY GRAHAM had just completed his sermon. His last words called upon his audience to come forward to receive Christ. For a moment no one in Seattle's vast new Kingdome stadium moved, and suddenly a small trickle of people began filing out of their seats and into the aisles. Soon what seemed like a small army of persons was headed across the field to a marked-off area in front of the plaform. As the inquirers came forward, a platoon of counselors moved into position. In a few moments each individual who had responded to Graham's invitation was greeted by a counselor who provided written material, prayer, encouragement, and the opportunity for lengthy discussion of the inquirer's spiritual status. This well-organized effort is one of the features of a Billy Graham crusade, and in a sense climaxes the months and even years of preparation which go into the creation of just one crusade.

Normally Graham is invited to a city by a group of ministers and laymen who have banded together out of a common wish to reach the community with the gospel message. He receives hundreds of such invitations every year. Graham and his associates evaluate these invitations. Each one is considered in terms of the specific needs of the community, the time involved, local interest in a crusade, the facilities available—including arena or stadium—and the usual weather conditions at the time the meeting is to be held. After much prayer and research an agreement is reached by the organization as to whether an invitation should be accepted or rejected. The final decision, however, comes from Billy Graham himself.

Once a city is included in the crusade schedule and a date has been confirmed, one of Graham's key associates moves to the community to act as crusade director. The director sets up an office, alerts the local leadership to the procedures of the organization, and gives leadership in the development of the crusade. The preparation period for a crusade can last anywhere from six months to two years. The crusade is administered by an executive committee made up of local ministers and lay people. The executive committee is responsible for the coordina-

tion of the crusade and for the delegation of responsibilities, including prayer, counseling, follow-up, and
finances. The subject of crusade financing is particularly important, since each crusade is expected to
pay for itself out of offerings and special gifts raised
within the community.

Since the primary objective of any Graham crusade is to bring individuals into a personal relationship with Christ and to firmly establish them in a
local church, the areas of counseling and follow-up
are especially important. Counselors are recruited
from local churches and undergo a four-week training program. The counselors are selected on the
basis of their personal faith, attendance at the counseling classes, completion of class assignments, and a
personal interview. When the counselor arrives at
the nightly crusade sessions he is given a specific
assignment, and it is his responsibility to determine
the spiritual needs of the individual who comes forward at Mr. Graham's invitation. The counselor attempts to guide the person to make a decision for
Christ, but he does not in any way influence a person
toward a specific church or denomination. He does
complete a card listing the inquirer's name, address,
and church affiliation. The counselor is directly responsible for contacting the inquirer within forty-
eight hours of his decision. The same night a person
comes forward at a rally, his name is sent to a local
church in his neighborhood. The local pastor is then
asked to report on the individual who has been

referred to his congregation. At the same time, the inquirer, who had been given a Bible study booklet at the time of his original commitment, is given the opportunity to continue studying the Scriptures through correspondence. The counseling and follow-up methods were developed by the Graham organization after years of research and experimenting. Very early in his ministry Graham realized that a process of follow-up had to be developed if people were to grow in their Christian faith. One of his associates recalls a crusade held in a Southern city early in Graham's career. "At the close of the sermon I found myself surrounded by hundreds of anxious souls needing instruction and guidance in the Word. After personally leading six men to Christ, I was humbled at seeing scores of people leaving the field without anyone to speak to them." The beginnings of Graham's solution to the problem came through the efforts of Dawson Trotman, the leader of an evangelical organization known as the Navigators, who had devised successful methods of helping servicemen with Christian commitment. Trotman worked with the Graham team and provided a valuable foundation upon which the later and more refined Graham counseling and follow-up techniques were based. Graham's follow-up system was aided by the talents of associates such as Charles Riggs and Dan Piatt, who would come into a city and spend months training crusade workers. The Graham follow-up program has been a genuine contribution to the field of evangelism, since in earlier days the evangelist usually came into a community, held a series of meetings, made converts, and promptly left without any follow-up. Today, there are thousands of people regularly attending evangelical churches who owe their firm spiritual base to the Graham organization's systematic counseling and follow-up program.

Not everyone, of course, agrees with Graham's activities. During the early 1970s Graham's crusades received mixed reactions from the media. Roy Larson, the religion editor of the influential *Chicago Sun Times,* criticized Graham for being "a very good-natured prophet of doom." He described Graham as "the bland leading the bland," and said that anyone who "ventures to write a dispassionate critique of the evangelist and his efforts runs the risk of appearing sacriligious." Larson had carefully observed Graham during the 1971 Chicago Crusade held at the mammoth McCormick Place. Larson felt that Graham's meetings were too predictable in nature and that he failed to "address himself to the sins of his own constituency." "Most of the time," Larson continued, "Graham appears to be talking over the heads of his immediate audience to those others not in the fold who are held accountable for a variety of sins of the spirit and of the flesh. As a result Graham often sounds like the small town newspaper editor accused by a critic of telling his readers what they already believe and then urging them to believe it. The burden of changing is placed on the others and the self-righteousness of the in-group is reinforced." In his concluding remarks on the Chicago Crusade, Larson raised the question, "Is Graham converting people to mainstream biblical Christianity or to mainstream Americanism?"

Over the years there has definitely been a tendency for the big-city, Northern press to be critical of Graham, while the Bible Belt media tend to look upon Graham's activities with favor. Thus, on the eve of Graham's Greater Southwest Crusade held in the fall of 1971 at Texas Stadium, home of the Dallas Cowboys football team, a long article in the *Dallas Times Herald* hailed Graham as "a super salesman for Christianity." The writer of the article described the evangelist as "a wonder to watch," and praised him for his humility, wittiness, and ability to explain his thoughts clearly. The *Dallas Times Herald* viewed Graham as a man of the people who reminds one of a big brother or favorite cousin, who is, on the one hand, not noticeable and on the other, scholarly enough "to be mistaken for a judge." The article went on to characterize Graham as a man who enlightens, reassures, and shatters unbelief. "Billy Graham is a super salesman, and his product is Christianity. He knows his product well, what he preaches he backs up with Scripture. His sermons are punctuated with such words as 'the Bible says,' 'Jesus says,' and 'according to the Scriptures.' " This article appeared in a special supplement and was accompanied by a series of stories welcoming Graham and his associates to the Texas city.

27.

Filmmaker and Author

THE GLITTERING CROWD of celebrities had just taken their seats in Los Angeles' ornate Beverly Theater, the scene of countless movie premieres, when the smell of teargas filled the theater. The 800 invited guests, who had come from all over the United States to attend the opening of the World Wide Pictures film, *The Hiding Place,* quickly left the theater and emptied into the streets. A squad of Los Angeles policemen soon found a four-inch canister near the theater's side entrance. This canister, which had a Nazi swastika emblem taped to its side, contained the teargas bomb. Billy Graham, who had been greeting last-minute arrivals in the theater lobby, was shocked by the incident and commented that this was a senseless act. *The Hiding Place* was the Graham organization's most ambitious film project, made at a cost of $1.7 million and shot on location in the Netherlands. The film told the story of Corrie ten Boom, a Dutch Christian woman, who with her family hid a number of Jewish people from Hitler's secret police during World War II. Most of Corrie's family, including her father and sister, died as a result of their heroic actions, and Corrie spent months in the infamous Ravensbruck concentration camp. Since the end of World War II Ms. ten Boom has toured the world proclaiming her faith.

Despite the adverse circumstances surrounding the premiere of the film, millions of people throughout the world eventually attended the showings and were exposed to Billy Graham's view that evil forces must be countered by noble actions.

Although he is best known as an evangelist and public speaker, Billy Graham is also an important filmmaker. World Wide Pictures, the filmmaking subsidiary of the Billy Graham Evangelistic Association, has produced more than 100 films. The first Graham film project, *Mr. Texas,* cost $25,000 to make, a far cry from the budget of some of Graham's latest film offerings. Originally the Graham films were shown in churches, but in recent years several World Wide Pictures features have been shown at neighborhood movie houses. Graham feels the use of film expands his evangelistic ministry and outreach and gives the opportunity for a dramatic portrayal of the gospel.

Graham also believes the printed word can be an important means of carrying the gospel message. Each month the Graham organization publishes the immensely popular *Decision* magazine. This attractive and highly readable periodical appears in ten English and foreign language editions and has a circulation approaching five million. The Graham organization encourages Christian writers, and each year workshops are held to help these authors better communicate their faith.

Billy Graham himself has been a busy author. He has published six major books and a number of shorter works. Over two million hardcover and paperback copies of his first book, *Peace with God,* have been distributed, and the book has been published in thirty-eight languages. During the middle 1960s his *World Aflame* sold more than a half-million copies. In one week alone over 29,000 books were shipped from his publisher to bookstores—breaking every record up to that time for either fiction or non-fiction in modern publishing history. In October of 1975 Graham's book *Angels: God's Secret Agents* was greeted by an avalanche of orders. Within less than a year the book had sold over one and a half million copies. He plans to follow up this book with a volume dealing with the Holy Spirit. Graham usually writes his books while on vacation. *Angels* was written during a visit to a friend's home in Mexico, and the final draft was put together at the evangelist's Montreat, North Carolina, home. In addition to writing occasional books and articles, Billy faces the continual pressure of preparing messages for his "Hour of Decision" radio broadcasts, his crusades, and the many other speaking assignments he takes on each year.

He is also the author of a daily column called "My Answer," which appears in hundreds of newspapers across the United States. These columns provide straightforward answers to questions sent in by readers.

28.

Love for the Human Family

THE SIGNS OF DEVASTATION were everywhere to be seen. Even now, three days after the earthquake struck Guatemala City, walls were tumbling down, water pipes were cracking, and after-shocks sent people running into the streets in fear. In response to one of the greatest national disasters ever to strike Central America, Billy and Ruth Graham left their vacation hideaway in Mexico and flew to Guatemala City for a first-hand investigation of the effects of this great natural disaster. Graham was not a curious tourist, rather he was in Guatemala to supervise the first efforts at rebuilding to be made by the Billy Graham Emergency Relief Fund, a relatively new arm of the evangelist's organization. The Fund had been started a few years before by Graham in an attempt to bring evangelicals into the forefront of social concern. Graham first announced the formation of the Fund at a crusade held in the twin cities of Minneapolis–St. Paul. Graham assigned his associate, Howard Jones, to direct the activities of the Emergency Relief Fund, and the initial grants were given to feed the hungry in Africa. The monies raised by the Fund are channeled through existing charitable and relief organizations, and every penny collected by the Fund is spent for either food, medicine, or other humanitarian purposes. When he established the Fund Graham was questioned as to why he was spending money on purposes other than a direct preaching of the gospel. Graham responded that Christians must be concerned about the welfare of the "whole man" and that it was well within the scope of the evangelistic ministry to care for the bodies of men as well as for their souls. Each check distributed by the Graham Relief Fund bears the inscription, "Given in the name of Jesus Christ."

The Fund, now a necessary part of the Graham Association's activities, shows how closely Graham has identified with historic evangelicalism. For although many American evangelicals in the twentieth century have been slow to understand and confront social issues, the evangelical movement has in the past made an important contribution to needed social reform. During the early part of the nineteenth century, evangelical Protestants in England, such as

William Wilberforce and John Newton, worked for the abolition of the slave trade and for prison reform. In America, the evangelist George Whitefield collected funds for orphans, blacks, and immigrants during his revival meetings. Many evangelicals were involved in the abolitionist movement. Oberlin College, which was headed by the outstanding mid-nineteenth century evangelist Charles G. Finney, was a particularly strong center of abolitionist activity.

Billy Graham, like his evangelical predecessors, has a genuine social conscience. He has a tremendous concern for people, and while his first priority is to lead them to Christ, he is also interested in their physical well-being.

At various times during Billy Graham's long and busy career, commentators have suggested that his influence has peaked and that he would soon disappear as an important public personality. In the 1960s one distinguished historian of American religion declared that Graham's "anti-intellectualism and individualistic emphasis" would cause him to step down from his role as leader of the nation's Protestants. This historian, of course, was wrong and, indeed, all predictions of Graham's public disappearance seem too early. The fact is that an increasing number of individuals, both in the United States and in many foreign nations, look to Graham for religious leadership, as well as for guidance on a wide range of moral and social issues. The turmoil of the 1960s and the uncertainties of the 1970s have made Graham an ever-more-important figure on the national and international scene. In the 1970s many Americans, touched by his honesty and the force of his personality, agreed with a well-known politician that Graham "is more than a preacher, more than an evangelist, more than a Christian leader. In a greater sense he has become our conscience."

In a time when so many political leaders and public personalities have been disgraced Graham remains an honest figure and an inspiration to tens of millions of people. In a time of instant heros, Graham's long career as a deeply respected leader is quite remarkable. For over thirty years he has captured the imagination and hearts of people representing the widest possible ethnic, national, and religious beliefs. He has been a faithful steward of the unique gifts granted him, and in this sense he has complied with the biblical injunction that from whom much is given, much is expected. He has advanced much farther along the road of real understanding than most of his evangelical contemporaries, and he remains a courageous and forceful leader willing to take risks and ready to engage in new ventures. More than any other single person he has made evangelical Christianity a respected and sought-after world-view, and there is little doubt that he will continue to be a force for good as long as his voice is heard throughout the nation and the world. He has met and advised presidents and kings and a host of famous people in all walks of life, but at heart he is the same humble person whose knees shook before his first major preaching assignment at Chicago's Orchestra Hall in 1944.

Epilogue

IT WAS GOOD to be in Charlotte. The warm spring day, bright sunshine, and soft, Southern air put the famous evangelist in an excited mood. As Graham walked toward the terminal to be greeted by the reception committee, happy memories of childhood days flooded his mind. He also thought of the millions of miles he had traveled since that first auto trip to Cleveland, Tennessee, and Bob Jones College. He had been to so many storied places. He had met famous persons, and in just a few moments another of these individuals, the President of the United States would arrive aboard Air Force 1 to participate in the ceremonies.

Billy deeply appreciated the honor which would soon be paid him, but he would have preferred getting into a car and driving the hundred miles to his house in Montreat. There he could spend quiet moments with Ruth, and he could rest, study, and prepare himself for the many journeys which lay ahead. In a few days he would head for Europe. In the fall he would travel to the Orient for meetings and crusades in Hong Kong and Taipei. A year from this day he would be busy helping his own nation recognize the spiritual roots which underlie her foundation and history.

As Billy Graham looked further ahead, he thought of the opportunity to spend more time writing, talking to young people, visiting with his own children and grandchildren. Yet in all of this, he was not anxious, nor did he have doubts about the future. He would live this day to the fullest, and in doing so he would be, as always, a faithful servant of the One to whom he had given his life in this same city so many years before.